My First Dictionary

Written by
Betty Root

Illustrated by
Jonathan Langley

DK

DORLING KINDERSLEY
London • New York • Stuttgart

DK

A DORLING KINDERSLEY BOOK

Editor Elizabeth Wilkinson
Art Editor Jane Horne

Managing Editor Jane Yorke
Managing Art Editor Chris Scollen
Production Jayne Wood

Photography by Steve Gorton,
Andy Crawford, Tim Ridley

First published in Great Britain in 1993
by Dorling Kindersley Limited,
9 Henrietta Street, London WC2E 8PS

Copyright © 1993 Dorling Kindersley Limited, London
6 8 10 9 7 5
Visit us on the World Wide Web at
http://www.dk.com

Photography (page 13 camel; page 33 goat and kid; page 40 jaguar;
page 44 leopard; page 91 zebra) copyright © 1991 Philip Dowell

A CIP catalogue record for this book is
available from the British Library

ISBN 0-7513-5024-9

Colour reproduction by Bright Arts, Hong Kong
Printed and bound in Italy by L.E.G.O., Vicenza

Contents

Note to parents and teachers 3

Note to parents and teachers

My First Dictionary is a colourful introduction to the world of words and their meanings for young children. Packed with photographs and lively artwork scenes, this book is designed to encourage children to practise using a dictionary, and to learn more about the language they use everyday.

About this book

Each of the 1,000 headwords featured in **My First Dictionary** has been carefully selected from words commonly used by young children. Every headword is clearly defined in simple language and further explained with a full-colour photograph or artwork. When teaching language and dictionary usage, it is essential to provide children with accurate visual clues to help them to identify the word they want. With this end in mind, every page of **My First Dictionary** has been tested in schools and adapted to suit the needs of young children.

Learning the alphabet

At the start, this dictionary will be a book to share with your child. Young children need to know the letters of the alphabet and understand alphabetical order as soon as they begin learning. This picture dictionary is an ideal tool for discovering how the alphabet works. Whilst you

are looking at the pictures in this book, point to the highlighted letter of the alphabet printed at the top of each page. Then point to each word as you name the pictures. In this way children will learn that there are groups of words that begin with the same letter, and sometimes the same sound.

Learning to read and spell

As children develop into more competent readers, they will enjoy using **My First Dictionary** independently. Children will be able to find out for themselves what a particular word means, or how to spell it. However, this goal is best achieved with the support and encouragement of caring adults.

Learning to use a dictionary

There is an exciting selection of word games at the back of this book. These games have been specially devised to help children to understand the purpose of a dictionary and to become confident users. By working through these language games together, you will encourage your child to learn dictionary skills through play.

To broaden children's vocabulary further, over 150 additional words - picked out in **bold** type in some of the dictionary definitions - are listed in the index. This listing provides young readers with the possibility of gaining cross-referencing skills that will enable them to work confidently with other dictionaries.

By looking at the pages of **My First Dictionary** with your children, you will provide them with a head start in reading and writing, and an enjoyable look at language.

Betty Root
Author

A

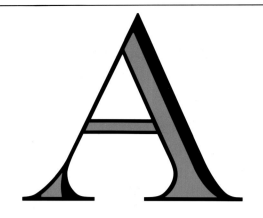

Aa Aa Aa Aa

above

When something is **above** something else, it is higher up. These birds are flying above the trees.

accident

An **accident** is something that happens by mistake.

acrobat

An **acrobat** is a person who can do gymnastics and clever balancing tricks. Some acrobats can balance on their heads or walk along on their hands.

act

To **act** is to pretend to be someone else. An **actor** is a person who acts in a play in front of an audience. Some actors act in television programmes and films.

add

To **add** is to find the sum total of two or more numbers.

address

Janet Brown
14 Elm Road
New Town

An **address** is the number of the building, and the name of the street and the town where a person lives or works.

adult

An **adult** is a grown-up person. Men and women are adults. When you are older, you will become an adult.

aeroplane

An **aeroplane** is a flying machine with wings. It flies people and packages quickly from one place to another.

airport

An **airport** is a place where aeroplanes take off and land.

alligator

An **alligator** is a reptile with thick, scaly skin and lots of sharp teeth.

alphabet

abcdefg
English alphabet

абвгдеж
Russian alphabet

An **alphabet** is a list of all the letters we use to write words. Different languages have different alphabets.

ambulance

An **ambulance** is a special vehicle that is used to carry sick or injured people to a hospital.

anchor

An **anchor** is a large, metal hook on a long chain. It digs into the bottom of the sea to stop a ship moving.

angry

An **angry** person is someone who feels very cross about something.

animal

An **animal** is any living thing that is not a plant. You are an animal, and so is a fish, a spider, a bird, a snake, and a dog.

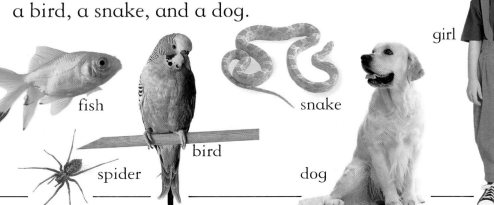

fish
spider
bird
snake
dog

ant

An **ant** is a tiny insect. Ants live in nests under the ground.

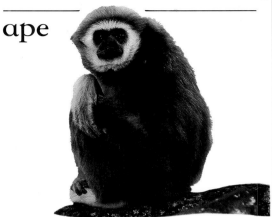

ape

An **ape** is a large monkey without a tail.

apple

An **apple** is a fruit that grows on an apple tree.

aquarium

An **aquarium** is a tank of water for keeping fish in. You can watch the fish as they swim around.

girl

arm

Your **arm** is the part of your body between your shoulder and your hand.

armadillo

An **armadillo** is an animal covered with hard, bony scales. These scales protect the armadillo from attack.

armour

Armour is a suit made of metal. Hundreds of years ago, soldiers wore armour to protect them in battle.

army

An **army** is a large group of soldiers who are trained to fight on land in times of war.

5

arrow

An **arrow** is a sign that points the way.

artist

An **artist** is a person who makes beautiful things. Some artists draw or paint pictures. Other artists make pots out of clay, or statues out of stone.

astronaut

An **astronaut** is a person who travels in outer space. Some astronauts have walked on the moon or launched space satellites.

athlete

An **athlete** is a person who is good at sports such as running, jumping, and swimming. Athletes take part in races or competitions.

audience

An **audience** is a group of people watching a play or listening to a concert.

author

An **author** is a person who writes stories, poems, or plays.

avalanche

An **avalanche** is a sudden fall of snow and rocks down the side of a mountain.

B

Bb *Bb* Bb *Bb*

baby

A **baby** is a very young child.

back

The **back** of something is the part behind the front.

back

Your **back** is the part of your body that is behind your chest. Your back is between your neck and your bottom.

bake

To **bake** something is to cook it in an oven. A **baker** is a person who makes bread and cakes in a **bakery**.

ball

A **ball** is used to play some games and sports. Most balls are round.

balloon

A **balloon** is a thin rubber bag that is blown up with air or another kind of gas.

banana

A **banana** is a long, curved fruit with a yellow skin. Bananas grow in bunches on banana plants.

band

A **band** is a group of people playing musical instruments together.

bandage

A **bandage** is a strip of material that is used to cover an injury.

bank

A **bank** is the high ground on both sides of a river or a stream.

bank

A **bank** is a safe place where you can keep money. You can take your money out again when you need it.

barbecue

A **barbecue** is a meal you cook outside on an open fire.

barn

A **barn** is a large farm building where a farmer keeps machinery or animals.

baseball

Baseball is a game played with a bat and ball by two teams of nine players.

basket

A **basket** is a kind of container for carrying things.

bat

A **bat** is a kind of stick that you use to hit a ball.

bat

A **bat** is a small, furry animal with wings. Bats hang upside down to sleep during the day. They hunt for food at night.

bath

A **bath** is a tub that you fill with water and sit in to wash yourself. A **bathroom** is the room where you take a bath.

battery

A **battery** is a sealed case that makes electricity for torches and toys.

beach

A **beach** is the strip of land by the edge of the sea. Beaches are covered with sand or pebbles.

beak

A **beak** is the hard, pointed part of a bird's mouth.

bear

A **bear** is a large, heavy animal with thick fur and strong claws.

beard

A **beard** is the hair that grows on a man's chin and cheeks.

bed

A **bed** is a piece of furniture that you sleep on. A **bedroom** is the room where you go to sleep.

bee

A **bee** is a flying insect. Some bees collect nectar, the sweet liquid in flowers, and turn it into honey.

beetle

A **beetle** is a flying insect. Beetles have hard, shiny wing cases to protect the soft parts of their bodies.

behind

When something is **behind** something else, it is at the back of it. This boy is hiding behind the curtains.

bell

A **bell** is a hollow piece of metal shaped like a cup. When you shake a bell, it rings.

below

When something is **below** something else, it is lower down. This bulb is growing below the surface of the soil.

belt

A **belt** is a strap that you wear around your waist.

bench

A **bench** is a seat for more than one person.

berry

A **berry** is a soft, juicy, stoneless fruit.

between

When you are **between** two things, you are standing in the middle of them.

bicycle

A **bicycle** is a machine with two wheels that are moved round by pedals. To ride a **bike** you sit on the seat, pedal with your feet, and steer using the handlebars.

handlebar

seat

pedal

wheel

big

When something is **big**, it is not small. This shirt is too big for this girl.

binoculars

Binoculars are a special kind of glasses. They make things that are far away look bigger and closer.

bird

A **bird** is an animal with feathers, two wings, and a beak. Most birds can fly.

birthday

Your **birthday** is the day of the year when you were born. You may get **birthday cards** and eat **birthday cake** on this special day.

bite

To **bite** something is to take hold of it with your teeth.

black

Black is a very dark colour. It is the opposite of white.

blanket

A **blanket** is a thick cloth that keeps you warm in bed.

blind

To be **blind** is to have difficulty seeing. **Guide dogs** help blind people to walk about safely.

blood

Blood is the red liquid that is pumped around your body by your heart.

blossom

Blossom is the flower that grows on a fruit tree.

blouse

A **blouse** is a garment worn by a girl or a woman on the top part of her body.

blow

To **blow** is to push air quickly out of your mouth. This girl is blowing bubbles.

blue

Blue is the colour of the sky on a sunny day.

boat

A **boat** is a small ship. Boats carry people and cargo across the water.

body

shoulder head

arm chest

leg hand

foot

Your body is every part of you.

bone

A **bone** is one of the pieces of a skeleton. You have 206 different bones in your body.

book

A **book** is a collection of pages held together between two covers. There are words and pictures printed on the pages of a book.

boomerang

A **boomerang** is a flat, curved piece of wood. When you throw a boomerang, it turns around in the air and comes back to you.

bottle

A **bottle** is a glass or plastic container for drinks and other liquids.

bottom

The **bottom** of something is the lowest part of it.

bowl

A **bowl** is a deep, round dish to put food in.

box

A **box** is a container with straight sides, a bottom, and sometimes a top.

boy

A **boy** is a male child.

brain

Your **brain** is inside your head. You think with your brain, and it controls your body.

branch

A **branch** is the part of a tree that grows from the tree trunk.

branch

tree trunk

bread

Bread is a food that is made from a mixture of water, flour or meal, and sometimes yeast.

break

When something **breaks**, it cracks into pieces.

breakfast

Breakfast is the first meal that you eat in the day.

brick

A **brick** is a block of baked, hard clay used for building.

bride

A **bride** is a woman who is getting married. The man she is marrying is the **bridegroom**. After the wedding, they are **wife** and **husband**.

bridge

A **bridge** is a road that is built over rivers or railways so that people can get across.

brown

Brown is a colour. Wood and soil are brown.

brush

A **brush** is a tool that has a lot of bristles. A **hair-brush** is used to brush your hair. Other kinds of brushes are used to sweep or paint with.

bucket

A **bucket** is a container with a handle that is used to hold water or other things.

bud

A **bud** is a young leaf or flower before it opens.

building

A **building** is a place, with walls and a roof, where people live or work. **Builders** use bricks, concrete, stones, or wood to **build** buildings.

bulb

A **bulb** is the part of a plant that grows underground.

bulb

A **bulb** is the glass part of an electric lamp that gives light.

bulldozer

A **bulldozer** is a powerful machine that is used to move heavy rocks and soil on a building site.

burglar

A **burglar** is a person who breaks into a building to steal something.

burn

To **burn** something is to set it on fire.

bus

A **bus** is a large vehicle that carries a lot of people. The **bus driver** stops at a **bus-stop** to let the passengers get on and off.

butcher

A **butcher** is a person who cuts up meat and sells it.

butter

Butter is a yellow, fatty food that is made from cream.

butterfly

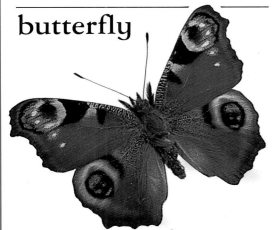

A **butterfly** is a flying insect with four colourful wings.

button

A **button** is a small, round object used for fastening clothes.

buy

To **buy** is to give money for something so that it belongs to you. The blond boy is buying a ball.

C

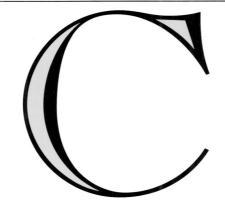

Cc Cc Cc Cc

cabbage

A **cabbage** is a vegetable with tightly packed leaves.

cabin

A **cabin** is a wooden house, often made from logs.

cactus

A **cactus** is a prickly plant that grows in the desert. A cactus stores water in its thick stem.

calculator

A **calculator** is a machine that you use to work with numbers.

calendar

A **calendar** is a chart that shows you what day it is. Calendars also show the month and the year.

camel

A **camel** is a large animal with one or two humps on its back. Camels live in hot, dry deserts.

camera

A **camera** is an instrument for taking photographs.

camp

To **camp** is to live outside. A **campsite** is a place where you set up your camping equipment.

carrot

A **carrot** is a long vegetable that grows underground.

can

A **can** is a sealed, metal container for storing food.

car

A **car** is a vehicle with four wheels and an engine. You travel in a car from one place to another. A **carpark** is a place where a lot of cars can park.

carry

To **carry** something is to take it from one place to another.

candle

A **candle** is a round stick of wax with a string through the middle. When you burn a candle, it gives off a bright light.

carnation

A **carnation** is a flower with a sweet smell and a lot of petals.

cassette

A **cassette** is a plastic container that stores sounds, like music, on special tape. You use a **cassette player** to listen to a cassette.

canoe

A **canoe** is a long, narrow boat that is moved through water with a paddle.

carpenter

A **carpenter** is a person who builds things out of wood. Some carpenters help to build houses. Other carpenters make furniture.

castle

A **castle** is a large building with thick, stone walls and tall towers. Castles were built hundreds of years ago to keep people safe from their enemies. Kings and queens lived in castles.

cap

A **cap** is a soft hat with a peak at the front.

cat

A **cat** is a furry animal that is often kept as a pet.

catch

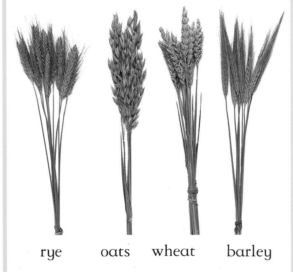

To **catch** is to grab hold of something as it comes towards you.

caterpillar

A **caterpillar** is a hairy insect with a long body.

cauliflower

A **cauliflower** is a vegetable with green leaves and a white centre.

cave

A **cave** is a large, dark hole in the side of a rock or under the ground.

centipede

A **centipede** is an insect with over 100 pairs of legs.

cereal

rye   oats   wheat   barley

Cereal is a kind of grass that is grown for its seeds. The seeds are used to make food like flour or breakfast cereal.

chair

A **chair** is a piece of furniture for one person to sit on.

chameleon

A **chameleon** is a type of lizard. It can change the colour of its skin to match the leaves and branches it is sitting on.

champion

A **champion** is a person who wins a sporting event or competition.

chase

To **chase** is to run after someone.

cheap

When something is **cheap**, you can buy it with a small amount of money.

checkout

A **checkout** is a cash-desk in a supermarket. Customers go through the checkout to pay for what they want to buy.

cheer

To **cheer** is to shout and wave your hands in the air with excitement.

cheese

Cheese is a food made from milk.

cheetah

A **cheetah** is a large, wild cat with a spotted coat. A cheetah can run faster than any other animal in the world.

chess

Chess is a game played on a chessboard.

chest

Your **chest** is the front part of your body, between your neck and your stomach.

chicken

cockerel

hen

chick

A **chicken** is a type of farm bird. A female chicken is called a **hen**. A male chicken is called a **cockerel**. A baby chicken is called a **chick**.

child

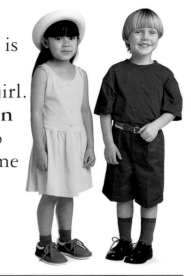

A **child** is a young boy or girl. **Children** grow up to become adults.

chimney

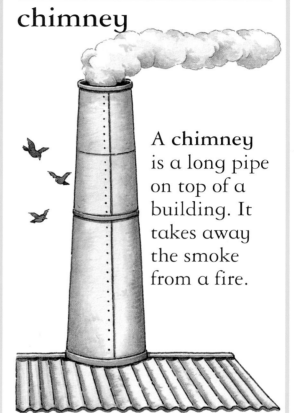

A **chimney** is a long pipe on top of a building. It takes away the smoke from a fire.

chimpanzee

A **chimpanzee** is a kind of ape. Chimpanzees live in family groups and play games together.

chin

Your **chin** is the part of your face below your mouth.

chocolate

Chocolate is a sweet bar made from cocoa and sugar.

choir

A **choir** is a group of people who sing together.

choose

To **choose** is to pick one thing instead of another.

chop-sticks

Chop-sticks are two thin sticks that you use to pick up and eat food.

church

A **church** is a building where Christian people meet to pray and to sing hymns.

circle

A **circle** is a type of shape. Circles are round.

city

A **city** is a large, important town with lots of buildings where people live and work.

clap

To **clap** is to bring your hands together and make a loud noise.

claw

A **claw** is the sharp, hooked nail on the foot of a bird or an animal.

clean

When something is **clean**, it is not dirty. One boot is clean, but the other is covered in mud.

cliff

A **cliff** is a high, steep rock near the sea. Waves crash against the cliffs.

climb

To **climb** is to go to the top of something using your hands and feet.

clock

A **clock** is a machine that shows you the time.

clothes

Clothes are the things that people wear. Clothes are usually made from cloth.

cloud

A **cloud** is made out of drops of water floating in the sky.

clown

A **clown** is a funny person who makes people laugh. Clowns wear colourful clothes and paint their faces.

coat

A **coat** is an item of clothing that you wear outside to keep yourself warm.

cobweb

A **cobweb** is a net made by a spider to catch flies.

cockpit

A **cockpit** is the part of an aeroplane where the pilot sits. All the controls for flying the aeroplane are in the cockpit.

coconut

A **coconut** is a fruit with a hard shell outside and coconut milk inside. Coconuts grow on coconut palms.

coffee

Coffee is a drink made from the brown seeds of the coffee bush. The seeds are called beans and are roasted and crushed to make a powder.

cold

When something is **cold**, it is not hot. When the weather is cold you may feel chilly and wear a coat.

colour

Red, blue, and yellow are **colours**. All other colours are a mixture of these colours.

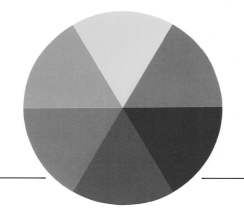

compact disc

A **compact disc** is a circle of flat plastic that stores a lot of sounds and pictures.
A **compact disc player** is a machine for playing some CDs.

computer

A **computer** is a machine that people use to write, to work with numbers, and to store information. You use a keyboard to call up the information on the screen.

conductor

A **conductor** is a person who keeps an orchestra playing together.

cone

A **cone** is a solid shape that is round at one end and pointed at the other.

continent

A **continent** is a large piece of land. We divide the world into seven continents: 1 Africa, 2 Antarctica, 3 Asia, 4 Australasia, 5 Europe, 6 North America, 7 South America.

cook

To **cook** is to heat food and get it ready to eat.

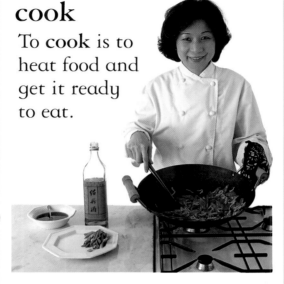

corner

A **corner** is the point where two lines meet. This shape has four corners.

cotton

Cotton is the white fibre that grows on a cotton-plant. Cotton is woven into cloth.

count

To **count** is to say numbers one after the other.

country

A **country** is a large area of land that is surrounded by borders and has its own laws. France is a country.

France

cousin

uncle
aunt
cousin

A **cousin** is a child of your aunt or uncle. An **aunt** is a sister of your mother or father. An **uncle** is a brother of your mother or father.

cow

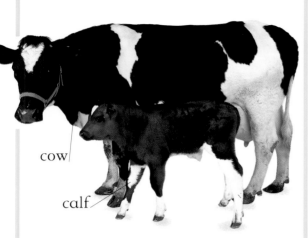

cow

calf

A **cow** is a large, farm animal that gives us milk to drink. Cows are female **cattle**. Male cattle are called **bulls** and young cattle are called **calves**.

crab

A **crab** is a sea animal with two claws and eight legs. Crabs have a hard shell to protect their soft bodies.

crane

A **crane** is a tall machine with a long arm that is used to lift heavy things.

crawl

To **crawl** is to move along on your hands and knees.

crayon

A **crayon** is a coloured pencil that you use for drawing.

cricket

Cricket is a team game that is played with a cricket bat and ball.

cricket

A **cricket** is a small insect that chirps by rubbing its legs together.

crocodile

A **crocodile** is an animal with large jaws and a powerful tail that helps it to swim.

crow

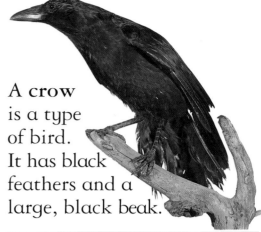

A **crow** is a type of bird. It has black feathers and a large, black beak.

crowd

A **crowd** is a large number of people squashed together in one place.

crown

A **crown** is a ring of gold and jewels that is worn on the head. Kings and queens wear crowns.

20

crutch

A **crutch** is a long, metal stick that helps you walk.

cup

A **cup** is a container that you drink out of.

cupboard

A **cupboard** is a piece of furniture with doors on the front. You store things on shelves in a cupboard.

D

Dd *Dd* Dd *Dd*

daffodil

A **daffodil** is a yellow spring flower that grows from a bulb.

cry

When you **cry**, tears run down your face. Crying shows that you are sad or hurt.

curtain

A **curtain** is a piece of material that hangs over or around a window. The curtain can be pulled across to cover the window.

daisy

A **daisy** is a flower with white petals and a yellow centre.

cube

A **cube** is a solid shape with six square sides.

cushion

A **cushion** is a bag full of soft material or feathers. We sit on cushions.

dam

A **dam** is a strong wall built across a river. A dam holds back water to make a lake.

cucumber

A **cucumber** is a long, thin vegetable with a green skin.

cut

To **cut** something is to slice it into pieces.

dance

To **dance** is to move your body in time to music.

dandelion

A **dandelion** is a yellow wild flower.

day

A **day** is 24 hours long. **Morning**, **afternoon**, **evening**, and **night** are all parts of one day.

morning   afternoon

evening   night

deaf

To be **deaf** is to have difficulty hearing. Some deaf people use sign language to talk to each other.

deer

A **deer** is a large, shy animal that can run very fast. A female deer is called a **doe**, and a young deer is called a **fawn**. Male deer are called **stags** and have antlers.

dentist

A **dentist** is a person who takes care of your teeth.

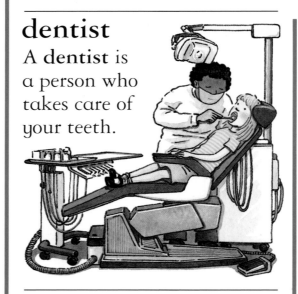

desert

A **desert** is a hot, dry, and sandy area of land.

desk

A **desk** is a type of table that you sit at to read and write.

dessert

A **dessert** is a sweet food that you eat at the end of a meal.

detective

A **detective** is someone who hunts for clues and solves crimes.

diagram

A **diagram** is a detailed drawing that explains how things work.

diamond

A **diamond** is a precious stone that sparkles. It is clear like glass.

diary

A **diary** is a small notebook in which you write what has happened in your day.

dictionary

A **dictionary** is a book with a list of words and their meanings arranged in alphabetical order. This book is a dictionary.

different

When two things are **different**, they are not the same.

dinner

Dinner is the main meal of the day.

dinosaur

A **dinosaur** is a huge animal that lived millions of years ago. Dinosaurs are now extinct.

dirty

When something is **dirty**, it is not clean. The dirty shoe is the one that is covered in mud.

disguise

A **disguise** is something you wear to hide who you are. Disguises make you look like someone else.

dive

To **dive** is to jump head first into water. A **diver** is a person who can dive.

doctor

A **doctor** is a person who helps sick or injured people to get well.

dog

A **dog** is a furry animal with a tail that wags. Dogs are often kept as pets.

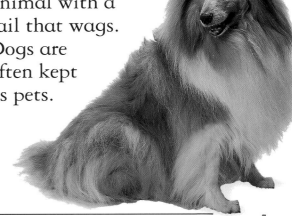

doll

A **doll** is a type of toy. Dolls look like babies or miniature people.

dolphin

A **dolphin** is an animal that lives in the sea. Dolphins are friendly and intelligent animals.

donkey

A **donkey** is an animal that looks like a small horse. Donkeys have long ears and a cross of fur on their backs.

door

A **door** is an entrance into a house or a room.

double

When something is **double**, it is twice as big or twice as many.

down

To move **down** is to go to a lower place. This train is travelling across the bridge and down the hill.

dragon

A **dragon** is an imaginary animal. Dragons have wings and they breathe fire.

dragonfly

A **dragonfly** is a flying insect with a long, thin body and four wings.

draw

To **draw** is to make lines that form a picture.

drawer

A **drawer** is a box that slides in and out of a **chest of drawers**.

dress

A **dress** is a garment worn by girls and women. The top and the skirt are joined together to make one piece.

dress

To **dress** yourself is to put on your clothes.

drill

A **drill** is a tool for making holes in wood, stone, or metal.

drink

To **drink** is to swallow a liquid such as juice or water.

drive

To **drive** a vehicle is to operate and steer it.
A **driver** is a person who can drive a vehicle.

drop

To **drop** something is to let it fall to the ground.

drum

A **drum** is a musical instrument that you play by tapping it with **drumsticks**.

dry

To **dry** your body is to rub away water with a towel.

duck

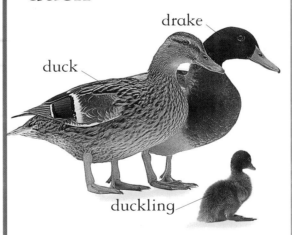

drake

duck

duckling

A **duck** is a type of bird that swims on water. Ducks have webbed feet and a flat beak. A male duck is called a **drake** and a baby duck is called a **duckling**.

dumper truck

A **dumper truck** is a lorry that is used to carry heavy loads of sand, soil, and stones.

E

Ee *Ee* Ee *Ee*

eagle

An **eagle** is a large, powerful bird of prey.

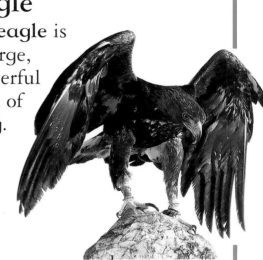

ear

Your **ear** is a part of your head. You have two ears for hearing.

Earth

The **Earth** is the planet on which we live. The Earth is our world.

easel

An **easel** is a stand for holding a picture whilst you paint it.

eat

To **eat** is to put food into your mouth, chew it, and swallow it.

egg

An **egg** is an unborn baby animal. Birds, insects, fish, and reptiles lay eggs. When an egg hatches, a baby animal comes out.

eight

Eight is the number that comes after seven and before nine.

elbow

Your **elbow** is the middle joint in your arm.

elbow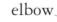

electricity

Electricity is a powerful force. Electricity makes machines work and gives us light and heat.

elephant

An **elephant** is a huge, grey animal with a long trunk, large floppy ears, and two tusks.

empty

Something that is **empty** has nothing in it.

emu

An **emu** is a large bird with long legs. Emus cannot fly, but they can run very fast.

engine

An **engine** is a machine that makes things move or run. All cars have engines.

engineer

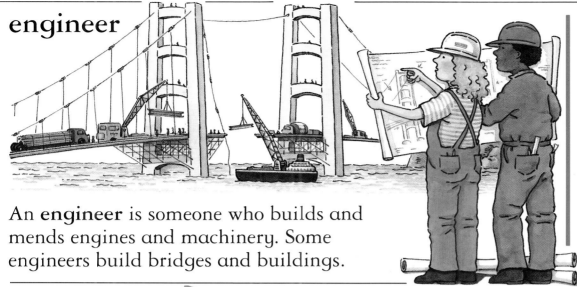

An **engineer** is someone who builds and mends engines and machinery. Some engineers build bridges and buildings.

exit

The **exit** is the way out of a building.

enter

To **enter** a building is to go into it through an **entrance**.

envelope

An **envelope** is a paper covering for a **letter**.

equator

The **equator** is an imaginary line around the Earth, halfway between the North and South Poles.

North Pole

South Pole

expensive

When something is **expensive**, it costs a lot of money to buy.

explode

When something **explodes**, it blows up and makes a loud noise.

equal

When things are **equal**, they are the same size, number, or weight as each other. These scales show that the red apples and green apples are equal in weight.

escalator

An **escalator** is a moving staircase.

exercise

To **exercise** is to make your body stronger and fitter. This boy is exercising his chest and arms.

eye

Your **eyes** are a part of your face. You have two eyes for seeing.

F

Ff *Ff* Ff *Ff*

fall

To **fall** is to drop to the ground.

face

Your **face** is the front part of your head. Your eyes, nose, and mouth are parts of your face.

forehead
eyebrow
eye
nose
mouth

factory

A **factory** is a building where a lot of people work together to make something.

fair

A **fair** is a place where people go to have fun. You can ride on a merry-go-round or a big wheel, and play games at the side-shows.

family

A **family** is a group of people who are related to each other. A **mother**, a **father**, a **brother**, and a **sister** are just one kind of family.

fan

A **fan** is a folded piece of paper that you wave to make a breeze.

farm

A **farm** is a piece of land for growing crops and keeping animals. A **farmer** is a person who works on a farm.

fast

When something moves **fast**, it moves very quickly. This top is spinning fast.

fat

When something is **fat**, it is not thin. One of these hamsters looks fat because its cheeks are packed with nuts.

feather

A **feather** is one of the light parts that covers a bird.

28

fight

To **fight** is to battle against someone or something.

film

A **film** is a thin strip of plastic that stores pictures. You can watch a film in a **cinema**.

finger

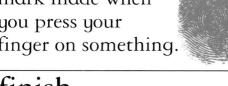

Your **finger** is a part of your hand. You have ten fingers.

fingerprint

A **fingerprint** is the mark made when you press your finger on something.

finish

To **finish** is to reach the end of something.

fire

A **fire** is heat, flames, and light made by something burning.

fire engine

A **fire engine** is a large truck that carries **fire fighters**, hoses, and a water pump to a fire.

first-aid

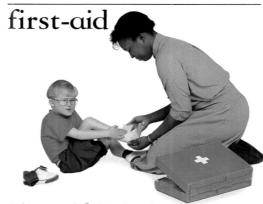

First-aid is the help given to an injured person before a doctor arrives.

fish

A **fish** is a kind of animal that lives in water.

fish

To **fish** is to try to catch a fish.

five

Five is the number that comes after four and before six.

flag

A **flag** is a symbol of a country, a club, or a group of people. It is made from a large piece of cloth with a pattern on it.

flipper

A **flipper** is a kind of arm on a sea-lion or a penguin. Flippers are used for swimming or moving along on land.

flipper

float

When something **floats**, it stays on top of water.

flute

A **flute** is a long, thin musical instrument. You play a flute by blowing across a hole at one end and pressing the keys with your fingers.

fog

Fog is a thick, grey cloud that hangs close to the ground.

flood

A **flood** is a great flow of water that goes over dry land.

fly

To **fly** is to move through the air like a bird, a kite, or an aeroplane.

fold

To **fold** something is to bend one part over the other part.

flour

Flour is a powder made from grain. It is used to make bread and cakes.

fly

A **fly** is a small, flying insect with two wings and six legs.

food

Food is all the things that we eat. Food gives us energy and helps our bodies to grow bigger and stronger.

flower

A **flower** is the colourful part of a plant or a tree. There are many different kinds of flowers.

foot

Your **foot** is the part of your body at the end of your leg. You have two **feet**.

football

American football

A **football** is a round or oval ball that is used to play a team game called **football**.

footprint

A **footprint** is the mark made by your shoe or foot on the ground.

forest

A **forest** is a large area of land where lots of trees grow.

fork

A **fork** is a tool that you use to pick up food.

fossil

A **fossil** is the remains of an animal or plant that lived millions of years ago. Fossils are found in rocks.

fountain

A **fountain** is a jet of water that shoots up into the air.

four

Four is the number that comes after three and before five.

fox

A **fox** is a wild animal that looks like a dog with a long, bushy tail.

friend

A **friend** is someone who you like a lot.

frog

A **frog** is an animal with webbed feet and strong back legs for jumping in and out of water.

fruit

A **fruit** is the juicy, seeded part of a plant.

frying-pan

A **frying-pan** is a wide, flat, metal cooking dish with a handle.

full

When something is **full**, it can hold no more.

fur

Fur is the thick, soft hair that grows on some animals and keeps them warm.

furniture

table

cupboard

bed

chair

Pieces of **furniture** are some of the moveable things in a house. Chairs and tables are pieces of furniture.

G

Gg Gg Gg Gg

game

A **game** is a competition with special rules.

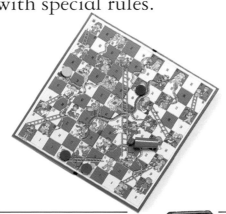

garage

A **garage** is a building where cars are parked.

garden

A **garden** is a place where lots of colourful flowers and vegetables are grown.

gate

A **gate** is a door in a fence or a wall.

ghost

A **ghost** is the spirit of a dead person. This is a pretend ghost.

giant

A **giant** is a huge, imaginary person.

giraffe

A **giraffe** is an animal with a very long neck and long, thin legs. Giraffes are the tallest animals in the world.

girl

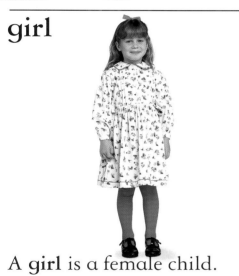

A **girl** is a female child.

give

To **give** is to hand something to someone.

glass

Glass is a hard material that you can see through. It breaks easily.

glasses

Glasses are worn over your eyes if you need help to see better.

globe

A **globe** is a round ball with a map of the world printed on it.

glove

A **glove** is a warm covering for your hand.

glue

Glue is a paste that you use to stick things together.

goal

A **goal** is two posts with a net or an empty space between them. In some games you kick a ball between the posts to score a goal.

goat

A **goat** is an animal with a beard under its chin and short horns. A female goat is called a **nanny goat**. A male goat is called a **billy goat**, and a young goat is called a **kid**.

nanny goat

kid

goggles

Goggles are special glasses that protect your eyes in the water.

gold

Gold is a precious, yellow metal that can be made into jewellery. Gold is found in rocks.

goldfish

A **goldfish** is a small, orange fish that is often kept as a pet.

golf

Golf is an outdoor game that is played with golf clubs and a golf ball. You use a club to hit a ball into a hole in the ground.

goose

A **goose** is a water bird with a short beak and a long neck. Male **geese** are called **ganders** and young geese are called **goslings**.

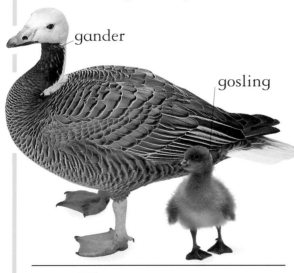

gander

gosling

gorilla

A **gorilla** is a big, strong ape.

grandparent

A **grandparent** is the parent of your mother or your father. Here are a **grandmother**, a **grandfather**, and their **grandchildren**.

grape

A **grape** is a small, round fruit that grows in a bunch on a grapevine.

grapefruit

A **grapefruit** is a round fruit with yellow skin.

grass

Grass is a green plant that covers the ground.

grasshopper

A **grasshopper** is a jumping insect with long, strong legs.

green

Green is a colour. Leaves are green in the summer.

grow

To **grow** is to get bigger.

guitar

A **guitar** is a musical instrument with a long neck and strings. You play a guitar by strumming or plucking the strings.

gymnast

A **gymnast** is a person who does special exercises in a **gymnasium**.

H

Hh *Hh* Hh *Hh*

hair

Hair is the soft covering that grows on your head and body.

half

A **half** is one of two equal parts. Two **halves** make a whole.

hammer

A **hammer** is a tool that you use for knocking in nails.

hand

Your **hand** is the part of your body below your wrist at the end of your arm. You hold things in your hand.

handle

A **handle** is the part of something that you hold.

hang

To **hang** something is to attach the top of it to a hook.

hangar

A **hangar** is a large building where aeroplanes are kept.

happy

A **happy** person is someone who feels pleased.

harbour

A **harbour** is a sheltered place, on a coast, where ships and boats are kept safely.

hat

A **hat** is a covering for your head.

hawk

A **hawk** is a bird of prey. Hawks eat small animals such as rabbits and fish.

head

Your **head** is the part of your body that is above your neck.

headlamp

A **headlamp** is the light on the front of a car or truck.

hearing-aid

A **hearing-aid** is a machine that you wear in your ear if you have difficulty hearing.

heart

Your **heart** is inside your chest. It pumps blood around your body.

heavy

If something is **heavy**, it weighs a lot and is difficult to move.

heel

Your **heel** is at the back of your foot.

ankle

heel

helicopter

A **helicopter** is a flying-machine that has large, spinning blades on top to lift it into the air.

helmet

A **helmet** is a hard hat that protects your head.

help

To **help** is to make someone's job easier.

hibernate

When an animal **hibernates**, it sleeps through the cold winter months. Dormice and squirrels hibernate.

hide

To **hide** is to put something in a place where no one can see it. This girl is hiding herself behind the easel.

high

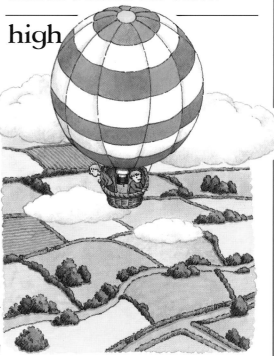

When something is **high**, it is not low. This hot-air balloon is high in the sky.

hill

A **hill** is a big hump in the land. Hills are smaller than mountains.

hip

Your **hip** is the bony part of your body that sticks out just below your **waist**. Your legs join your body at your hips.

hippopotamus

A **hippopotamus** is a large animal with very thick skin and short legs. It likes to wallow in muddy water.

hold

To **hold** something is to have it in your hands or arms.

hole

A **hole** is an opening in something.

honey

Honey is a sweet, sticky syrup that is made by bees.

hoof

A **hoof** is the hard covering on the feet of some animals.

hop

To **hop** is to jump up and down on one leg.

horn

A **horn** is something that makes a loud noise to warn people of danger.

horse

A **horse** is a large animal with a mane, a tail, and hooves. A female horse is called a **mare**, a male horse is called a **stallion**, and a baby horse is called a **foal**.

hospital

A **hospital** is a place where doctors and nurses take care of sick or injured people.

hot

When something is **hot**, it is not cold. When the weather is hot, the heat makes you feel very warm.

37

hotel

A **hotel** is a building with a lot of bedrooms. People pay to sleep and eat in a hotel.

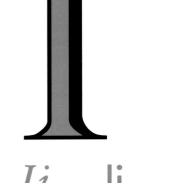

Ii *Ii* Ii *Ii*

house

A **house** is a building where people live.

hug

To **hug** is to put your arms around something and hold it tightly.

hundred

A **hundred** is the number that comes after 99 and before 101.

hutch

A **hutch** is a pet rabbit's house.

hyena

A **hyena** is a wild animal that looks like a wolf. A hyena's call sounds like a loud, human laugh.

ice

Ice is frozen water.

ice-cream

Ice-cream is a frozen dessert made from cream and eggs.

iceberg

An **iceberg** is a very large piece of ice that floats in the ocean.

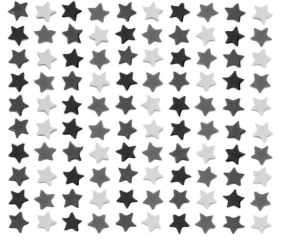

icicle

An **icicle** is a hanging piece of ice made by water freezing as it drips.

igloo

An **igloo** is a house made from blocks of snow and ice.

iguana

An **iguana** is a large lizard with a long tail and a ridge of spines along its back. Iguanas live in trees.

injection

An **injection** is a special way that a doctor or nurse can give you medicine quickly. A needle is pricked into your skin, and the medicine is pushed through the needle into your body.

injure

To **injure** yourself is to hurt yourself. This boy has had an accident. He has an **injury** to his ankle and he's in a lot of pain.

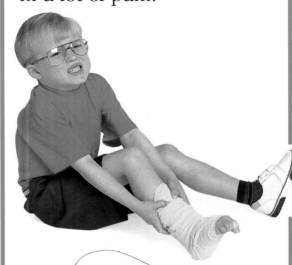

insect

An **insect** is a tiny animal with six legs and a hard shell.

inside

When something is **inside**, it is within and not outside. These shoes are inside a shoebox.

instrument

An **instrument** is something that makes musical sounds.

tuba

invent

To **invent** is to make something that did not exist before. An **inventor** invents things.

invite

To **invite** someone is to ask them to a party or another event. A **invitation** is the card that you send.

Please Come to My Party

iron

An **iron** is a hot tool that takes the creases out of clothes.

island

An **island** is a piece of land with water all around it.

ivy

Ivy is a plant that grows up walls and trees.

J

Jj *Jj* Jj *Jj*

jacket

A **jacket** is a short coat.

jaguar

A **jaguar** is a large, wild cat with a spotted coat.

jam

Jam is a sweet food that you spread on bread. It is made by boiling fruit with sugar.

jar

A **jar** is a glass container with a wide neck and a lid.

jaw

Your **jaw** is the bony part of your mouth that holds your teeth. You move your lower jaw when you chew.

jeans

Jeans are trousers made out of strong, blue cotton cloth.

jellyfish

A **jellyfish** is a sea animal with a soft body and long tentacles.

jewel

A **jewel** is a precious stone, like an emerald or a ruby. Jewels are used to make sparkling **jewellery** like these earrings.

jigsaw puzzle

A **jigsaw puzzle** is a picture cut up into pieces that you have to fit together again.

judo

Judo is a fighting sport using holds and throws.

jug

A **jug** is a container with a handle and a spout for pouring liquids.

juggle

To **juggle** is to keep several objects in the air by throwing and catching them quickly. A **juggler** is a person who can juggle.

juice

Juice is the liquid that comes out of fruit.

jump

To **jump** is to leap into the air so that both feet leave the ground.

jungle

A **jungle** is a hot, steamy forest where it rains a lot. There are lots of tall trees in a jungle. Jungles can be called **rainforests**.

K

Kk *Kk* Kk *Kk*

kangaroo

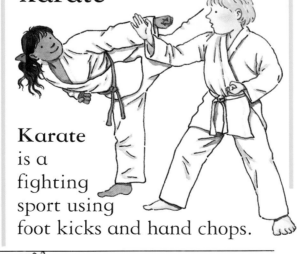

A **kangaroo** is an animal with long, powerful back legs, which it uses for jumping. A female kangaroo carries her baby in her pouch.

karate

Karate is a fighting sport using foot kicks and hand chops.

kennel

A **kennel** is a house for a pet dog.

key

A **key** is a metal tool for locking or unlocking doors.

kick

To **kick** is to hit out with your foot.

king

A **king** is a man who heads a country. Kings live in palaces.

kiss

To **kiss** is to touch someone with your lips.

kitchen

A **kitchen** is the room where food is cooked.

knit

To **knit** is to knot wool to make a sweater or a scarf. You knit with knitting-needles.

kite

A **kite** is a toy that you fly in the wind.

kneel

To **kneel** is to go down on your knees.

knock

To **knock** is to tap something with your knuckles to make a noise.

kitten

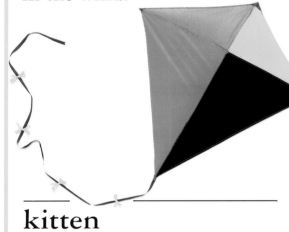

A **kitten** is a young cat.

knife

A **knife** is a tool with a sharp blade used for cutting.

knight

A **knight** is a brave soldier who lived hundreds of years ago. Knights wore suits of armour.

knot

A **knot** is a fastening made by tying things together. This is a knot in a piece of rope.

knee

Your **knee** is the joint in the middle of your leg. Your leg bends at your knee.

koala

A **koala** is a furry animal with big ears and a black nose. Koalas eat eucalyptus leaves and live in trees.

L

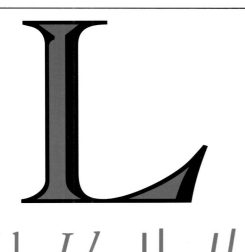

Ll *Ll* Ll *Ll*

laboratory

A **laboratory** is a place where people learn about science, and do experiments.

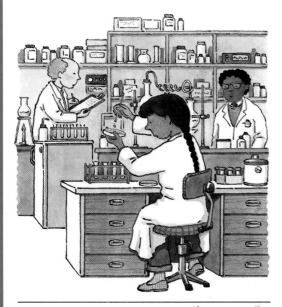

ladder

A **ladder** is a tall climbing frame with lots of steps. You climb ladders to reach high places.

ladybird

A **ladybird** is a tiny insect that often has spotted wing cases.

lake

A **lake** is a large area of water surrounded by land.

lamb

A **lamb** is a young sheep.

lamp

A **lamp** is a stand for a bulb that is covered by a lampshade. A lamp gives off light.

land

Land is the part of the Earth that is not sea. We walk on land.

large

When something is **large**, it is not little. This large doll contains all the little dolls.

laugh

To **laugh** is to make sounds that show you are happy.

lawn

A **lawn** is a piece of ground that is covered with grass. A lawn is cut with a **lawnmower**.

leaf

A **leaf** is a flat, green part of a plant that grows from its stem.

lean

To **lean** is to tilt your body to one side.

leopard

A **leopard** is a wild cat with sharp teeth and claws. Leopards have a yellow coat with black spots.

lick

To **lick** something is to touch it with your tongue.

left

Left is the opposite of right. This girl is about to make a left turn on her bicycle.

letter

A **letter** is a part of the alphabet. You put letters together to make words.

lifeboat

A **lifeboat** is a type of boat that is used to rescue people out at sea.

leg

Your **leg** is the part of your body between your bottom and your foot. People walk on two legs.

lettuce

Lettuce is a leafy, green vegetable that you eat in a salad.

lift

To **lift** something is to pick it up.

lemon

A **lemon** is a yellow fruit with a very sour taste.

library

A **library** is a place where lots of books are kept on shelves. You can borrow books to read from some libraries.

light

If something is **light**, it is not heavy. Light things weigh very little and are easy to lift.

lighthouse

A **lighthouse** is a tall tower by the sea with a bright light on the top. Lighthouses warn ships of danger.

lightning

Lightning is a flash of light that appears in the sky during a **thunderstorm**.

lion

A **lion** is a fierce big cat that roars. A male lion has a shaggy mane around its head. A female lion is called a **lioness**.

lioness

lion

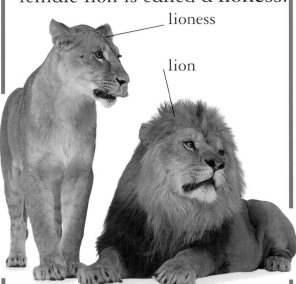

lip

Your **lips** are the soft, fleshy edges around your mouth.

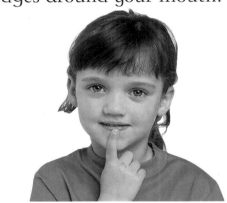

liquid

A **liquid** is wet and can be poured like this water.

litter

Litter is the wastepaper and other rubbish that should be put in a wastepaper-basket.

little

When something is **little**, it is not large. Little things are small in size like this purple flower.

lizard

A **lizard** is a reptile with a long, scaly body, a tail, and four short legs.

lobster

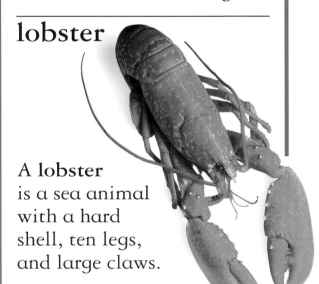

A **lobster** is a sea animal with a hard shell, ten legs, and large claws.

lock

A **lock** is a fastening that you open with a key. This is a padlock.

log

A **log** is a thick piece of wood that has been cut from a tree.

long

When something is **long**, it measures a lot from end to end. One of these strings of beads is much longer than the other.

look

To **look** is to use your eyes to see things.

lose

When you **lose** something, you cannot find it. This girl has lost a shoe.

love

To **love** is to like someone or something very much.

low

When something is **low**, it is not high. This girl is low down in the grass.

luggage

Luggage is all the bags and cases that you take on holiday.

lunch

Lunch is the meal that you eat in the middle of the day.

lung

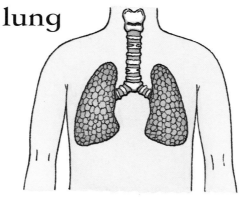

Your **lung** is inside your chest. You have two lungs for breathing.

M

MmMmMmMm

machine

A **machine** is an object with parts that move together to make something work. Clocks, cars, bicycles, and computers are all machines.

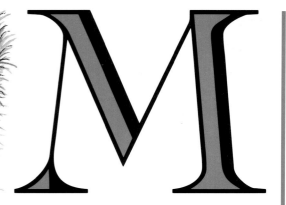

magazine

A **magazine** is a thin book that you buy each week or month.

magic

Magic is a way of doing amazing tricks that seem to be impossible. A **magician** is a person who can do magic tricks.

magnet

A **magnet** is a piece of iron or steel that can pull other pieces of iron or steel towards it.

magnifying glass

A **magnifying glass** is a special piece of glass that makes things look bigger than they really are.

mammal

A **mammal** is any warm-blooded animal that feeds on its mother's milk.

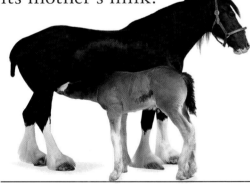

man

A **man** is a grown-up boy.

map

A **map** is a drawing of part of the Earth's surface. This map of the world shows where the countries are.

market

A **market** is a place where people buy and sell things from stalls.

mask

A **mask** is a covering for your face. You wear a mask to disguise yourself.

match

A **match** is a short stick that makes a flame when you rub it on a rough surface.

mathematics

Mathematics is the study of numbers, shapes, and sizes.

meal

A **meal** is the food that you eat at one time.

measure

To **measure** something is to find out what size it is.

meat

Meat is the part of an animal that is eaten as food.

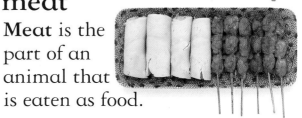

mechanic

A **mechanic** is a person who makes and repairs cars or other machines.

microscope

A **microscope** is an instrument that makes tiny things look bigger.

medal

A **medal** is a piece of metal, usually shaped like a large coin. Medals are given to people who win competitions.

melt

When something **melts**, it turns to liquid as it warms up.

metal

Metal is a hard material like copper, iron, or steel. Metals are found in rocks.

microwave oven

A **microwave oven** is a machine for cooking food very quickly.

medicine

Medicine is a pill or a liquid that you take to make you better if you are ill.

midday

Midday is the middle of the day. You eat your lunch at midday.

meet

To **meet** someone is to come face to face with them.

microphone

A **microphone** is an instrument that makes your voice sound louder.

midnight

Midnight is the middle of the night. You are asleep at midnight.

milk

Milk is a white liquid that some animals make to feed their babies. Many people drink cow's milk.

mine

A **mine** is a deep hole under the ground where people dig for rocks like coal.

mineral

A **mineral** is a part of the rock that is dug out of a mine.

mirror

A **mirror** is a special piece of glass in which you can see your reflection.

mix

To **mix** things is to stir them together.

money

Money is the coins and paper notes that we use to buy things.

monkey

A **monkey** is a furry animal with long arms, fingers, and toes. Monkeys have tails to help them to swing in trees.

monster

A **monster** is a strange, frightening creature that you read about in fairy tales.

month

A **month** is a measure of time that is about 30 days long. There are 12 months in a year.

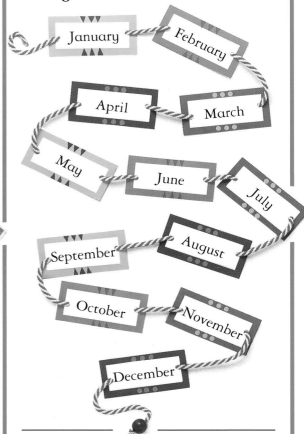

January
February
April
March
May
June
July
September
August
October
November
December

moon

The **moon** is the Earth's satellite. It shines in the sky at night.

mosaic

A **mosaic** is a picture made by fitting together coloured pieces of stone or glass.

mosque

A **mosque** is a building where Muslim people meet to pray.

mosquito

A **mosquito** is a flying insect that bites your skin to suck your blood.

moth

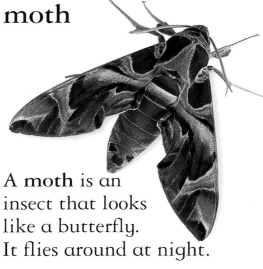

A **moth** is an insect that looks like a butterfly. It flies around at night.

motorbike

A **motorbike** is a machine that you ride. This motorbike has a powerful engine.

mountain

A **mountain** is a very high, rocky hill.

mouse

A **mouse** is a small, furry animal with a long tail. **Mice** live in nests.

moustache

A **moustache** is the hair that grows above a man's lips.

mouth

Your **mouth** is part of your face. You use your mouth for eating and speaking.

mud

Mud is wet, soft earth.

muscle

Muscle is the part of your body that gives you strength to move and to lift things.

museum

A **museum** is a building where you can see old and fascinating things.

mushroom

A **mushroom** is a fungus that is shaped like a small umbrella. You can eat some mushrooms, but others are poisonous.

music

Music is the notes that you read, or the sound that you make, when you are singing or playing an instrument.

musician

A **musician** is a person who can make music by playing a musical instrument.

N

Nn *Nn* **Nn** *Nn*

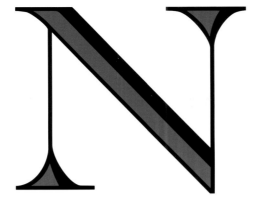

nail

A **nail** is a small, metal spike with a sharp point at one end. You hammer nails into wood.

narrow

When something is **narrow**, it is not wide. Narrow spaces are difficult to squeeze through.

navy

A **navy** is a large group of warships carrying sailors who are trained to fight at sea in times of war.

neck

Your **neck** is the part of your body that is between your head and your shoulders.

needle

A **needle** is a thin, pointed piece of metal that you use for sewing.

nest

A **nest** is a home where an animal lives and cares for its babies.

net

Net is material made from loosely knotted string. You can catch fish in a net.

new

When something is **new**, it is not old. New things have just been made or bought.

newspaper

A **newspaper** is big sheets of paper with words printed on them. You read the newspapers to find out about world events.

newt

A **newt** is an animal that lives in or around water.

night

Night is the time when it is dark outside. Night begins at sunset and ends at sunrise.

nine

Nine is the number that comes after eight and before ten.

noise

A **noise** is a loud sound. This boy is making a noise, on his drum.

nose

Your **nose** is part of your face. You breathe through your nose.

number

A **number** is a sign that tells you how many things there are.

nurse

A **nurse** is a person who is trained to take care of sick or injured people in a hospital.

nut

A **nut** is a small piece of metal that you screw on to a **bolt**. Nuts and bolts are used to hold things together.

nut

bolt

nut

A **nut** is a fruit with a hard shell and a soft inside that you can eat.

nutcracker

A **nutcracker** is a tool for breaking open nuts.

O

Oo Oo Oo Oo

office

An **office** is a place where people go to work. There are desks, chairs, computers and filing cabinets in offices.

oar

An **oar** is a long pole with a flat blade at one end. You use oars to row a boat.

ocean

An **ocean** is a large body of salt water. The Pacific and the Atlantic are oceans.

octopus

An **octopus** is a sea animal with eight long arms and a soft, round body.

oil

Oil is a greasy liquid that makes machines run smoothly.

old

When something is **old**, it is not new. Old things look used.

one

One is the number that comes before two. When you count, you start with the number one.

onion

An **onion** is a round vegetable that makes your eyes water when it's cut open.

open

When something is **open**, it is not shut or closed.

opera

An **opera** is a play in which the words are sung to music.

53

opposite

When things are the **opposite** of each other, they are completely different. Hot and cold are opposites, so are front and back.

optician

An **optician** is a person who makes or sells glasses.

orange

Orange is a colour made by mixing red and yellow.

orange

An **orange** is a round, juicy fruit with a thick, orange-coloured skin.

orangutan

An **orangutan** is a large ape with long fur, and strong arms.

orchard

An **orchard** is an area of land where fruit-trees are grown.

orchestra

An **orchestra** is a large group of musicians playing instruments together.

organ

An **organ** is a musical instrument with a keyboard, and long metal pipes that make sounds when air is pushed through them.

ostrich

An **ostrich** is a large bird with a long neck, long legs, and lots of big feathers. Ostriches cannot fly, but they can run very fast.

otter

An **otter** is a furry animal that lives in or near water.

outside

When something is **outside**, it is not inside. This puppy is outside its kennel.

oval

An **oval** is a type of shape. Eggs are oval.

oven

An **oven** is a machine for cooking food.

owl

An **owl** is a bird with a large head, and big, round eyes. Owls usually hunt for food at night.

oyster

An **oyster** is a sea animal with a soft body inside a hard shell. Some oysters make pearls inside their shells.

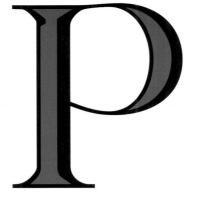

P

Pp *Pp* Pp *Pp*

page

A **page** is one side of a sheet of paper in a book.

paint

To **paint** is to make a picture using a brush and paints.

paint

Paint is a coloured liquid used to paint pictures.

pair

A **pair** is a set of two things that are used together, like shoes or socks.

palace

A **palace** is a very large, grand house where kings and queens live.

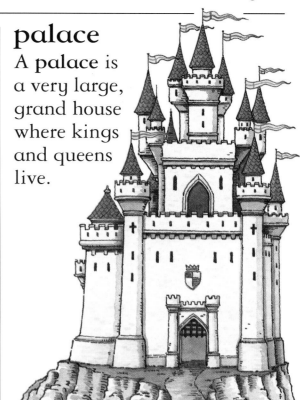

palm

Your **palm** is the inside part of your hand.

palm tree

A **palm tree** is a tree that grows in hot countries. Palm trees have large leaves that grow at the top of a long trunk.

panda

A **panda** is a large, furry animal. Giant pandas look like bears with black and white fur.

panther

A panther is a large leopard with a black coat.

parent

A parent is a person who has a child. Your mother and father are your parents. You are their **son** or **daughter**.

passenger

A passenger is a person who travels in a bus or a car. Passengers do not do the driving.

paper

Paper is a material you use to write on.

park

A **park** is a piece of land where people can enjoy the gardens and playgrounds.

path

A **path** is a track for people to walk on.

parachute

A **parachute** is a large piece of material that is shaped like an umbrella. Parachutes help people to float through the air and land safely on the ground.

parrot

A **parrot** is a bird with brightly coloured feathers. Some parrots can be trained to repeat words.

patient

A **patient** is a person who is ill and is being cared for by a nurse or a doctor.

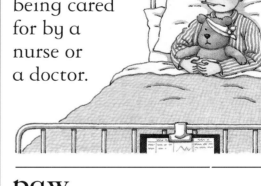

paw

A **paw** is an animal's foot.

parcel

A **parcel** is something that is wrapped in paper.

party

A **party** is a group of friends having lots of fun together. You might have a party on your birthday.

pay

To **pay** for something is to give money for it. The girl is paying the shopkeeper.

pea

A **pea** is a small, round vegetable that grows in a pod.

peach

A **peach** is a sweet, juicy fruit with a soft skin, and a stone in the middle.

peacock

A **peacock** is a bird with colourful tail feathers that open out like a fan.

peanut

A **peanut** is a seed that grows in a pod in the soil.

pear

A **pear** is a fruit that narrows at the top and has pips in the middle.

pearl

A **pearl** is a small, white gemstone that is found in some oyster shells. Pearls are used to make jewellery.

pebble

A **pebble** is a small, smooth stone found on the beach.

peel

Peel is the skin of some fruits and vegetables.

peel

To **peel** something is to take the skin off it. This girl is peeling an orange.

pelican

A **pelican** is a bird with a large pouch under its beak for catching fish to eat.

pen

A **pen** is a tool filled with ink used for writing.

pencil

A **pencil** is a tool made from wood and lead. You use a pencil to write and to draw.

penguin

A **penguin** is a black and white sea bird that cannot fly. Penguins use their short wings to swim in the water.

people

People are **men**, **women**, and children.

pepper

Pepper is a powder made from the dried berries of a pepper plant. You use pepper to flavour food.

perfume

Perfume is a sweet-smelling liquid made from flower petals. You put perfume on your body.

pet

A **pet** is a tame animal that you take care of and keep at home as a friend.

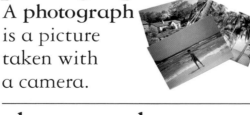

petal

A **petal** is a coloured part of a flower.

photograph

A **photograph** is a picture taken with a camera.

photographer

A **photographer** is a person who takes photographs.

piano

A **piano** is a large musical instrument with black and white keys. You press the keys to make music.

picnic

A **picnic** is a meal that you eat outside.

picture

When you make a **picture**, you draw or paint what something looks like.

pie

A **pie** is a pastry case filled with fruit, meat, or vegetables, and baked in an oven.

pig

piglet

A **pig** is an animal with a short snout, a little tail, big ears, and bristly hairs on its skin. A male pig is called a **boar**. A female pig is called a **sow**, and a baby pig is called a **piglet**.

pigeon

A **pigeon** is a bird with a large, round body and a small head. Some pigeons live in cities.

pile

A **pile** is a lot of things stacked on top of one another.

pillow

A **pillow** is a bag of soft material for your head to rest on.

pilot

A **pilot** is a person who flies an aeroplane.

pin

A **pin** is a short, thin piece of metal used to hold cloth together.

pineapple

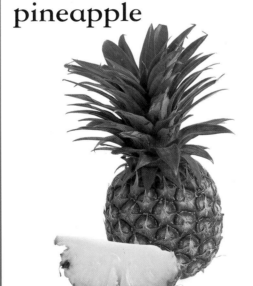

A **pineapple** is a large fruit with thick, bumpy skin and pointed leaves. The fruit inside is sweet and juicy.

pink

Pink is a colour. It is made by mixing red and white.

pipe

A **pipe** is a hollow tube of metal or plastic. Liquid runs through pipes.

pirate

A **pirate** is a robber who steals from ships at sea.

planet

A **planet** is a huge ball of rock, metal, and fire that moves around the sun. There are nine planets in space.

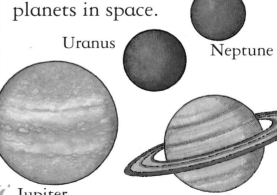

Pluto

Uranus

Neptune

Jupiter

Saturn

Mars

Earth

Mercury

Venus

plant

A **plant** is anything that grows in the soil. Flowers and trees are plants.

plastic

Plastic is a material made from chemicals. This blow-up toy is made out of plastic.

plate

A **plate** is a flat dish that you put food on.

play

To **play** is to have fun.

plum

A **plum** is a purple fruit with a stone in the middle.

plumber

A **plumber** is a person who works on water or gas pipes.

pocket

A **pocket** is a small bag that is sewn into your clothes.

point

A **point** is the sharp end of something. These objects all have sharp points.

polar bear

A **polar bear** is a huge bear covered in thick, white fur.

police officer

A **police officer** is a person who keeps law and order.

polish

To **polish** is to rub something to make it shine.

pond

A **pond** is a small lake.

pony

A **pony** is a small horse.

poppy

A **poppy** is a flower with big red, orange, yellow, or white petals.

porcupine

A **porcupine** is an animal with pointed hairs called quills.

post office

A **post office** is a place where you can buy stamps, and post letters and parcels. A **postal worker** is someone who works in a post office.

potato

A **potato** is a vegetable that grows in the ground.

pour

To **pour** a liquid is to tip it out of a container.

prawn

A **prawn** is a sea animal with a hard shell and long antennae.

present

A **present** is a parcel that you give to someone on a special occasion.

price

The **price** of something is the amount of money you have to pay for it.

£10·50

prickle

A **prickle** is a sharp point, like the ones on this chestnut.

prince

A **prince** is the son of a king and queen. A **princess** is the daughter of a king and queen.

prize

A **prize** is a reward you may be given if you win a competition.

pump

A **pump** is a machine that pushes liquid or air into something. This pump pushes air into a bicycle tyre.

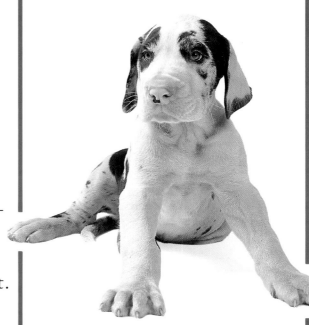

puppy

A **puppy** is a young dog.

propeller

A **propeller** is the blades that spin round to power aeroplanes or boats.

puncture

A **puncture** is a small hole, in a tyre, that lets the air out.

purple

Purple is a colour. It is made by mixing blue and red.

puddle

A **puddle** is a pool of muddy water.

pupa

A **pupa** is a caterpillar changing into a butterfly or a moth.

push

To **push** is to take hold of something and move it away from you.

pull

To **pull** is to take hold of something and move it towards you.

puppet

A **puppet** is a doll that is moved by strings or your fingers.

puzzle

A **puzzle** is a game or a problem that you enjoy trying to work out.

pyramid

A **pyramid** is a building with a square base and sloping, triangular sides. Ancient peoples built pyramids.

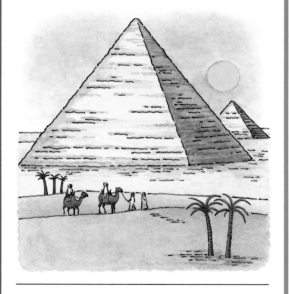

python

A **python** is a large snake that kills its prey by squeezing it to death.

Q

Qq Qq Qq Qq

quarry

A **quarry** is a place where stone is cut out of the ground. The stone is used for building.

quarter

A **quarter** is one of four equal parts. Four quarters make a whole.

queen

A **queen** is a woman who heads a country. Queens live in palaces.

quick

To be **quick** is to do something in a short time.

quiet

To be **quiet** is to make no noise at all.

quilt

A **quilt** is a warm, soft covering for a bed.

quiz

A **quiz** is a game in which people try to answer lots of questions.

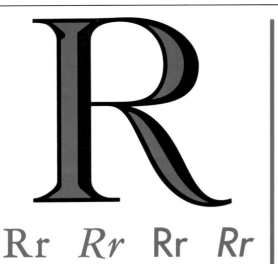

R

Rr *Rr* Rr *Rr*

radio

A **radio** is a machine that receives sound waves from the air. It turns them into music or voices that you can listen to.

rain

Rain is drops of water that fall from clouds in the sky.

rabbit

A **rabbit** is a small, furry animal with long ears.

raft

A **raft** is a flat boat that is made out of logs.

rainbow

A **rainbow** is an arc of different colours that appears in the sky when the sun shines through rain. The seven colours of the rainbow are: red, orange, yellow, green, blue, **indigo**, and **violet**.

race

A **race** is a competition to find out who is the fastest.

railway

A **railway** is a track for trains to run along. The track is made from long strips of metal called **rails**.

reach

railway station

A **railway station** is a place where you go to buy a ticket and catch a train.

To **reach** for something is to stretch out your hand to take or touch it. This boy is reaching for his toys.

racing car

A **racing car** is a type of car that goes very fast around a track.

read

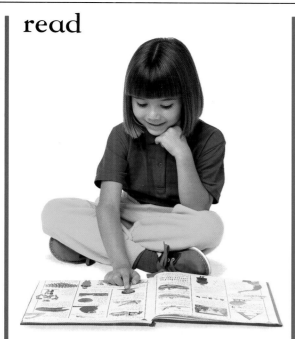

To **read** is to understand the meaning of written or printed words.

record

A **record** is a circle of flat plastic that stores sounds like music. You use a **record player** to listen to a record.

recorder

A **recorder** is a wooden or plastic musical instrument. You play a recorder by blowing down it and covering the holes with your fingers.

rectangle

A **rectangle** is a shape with two long sides, two shorter sides, and four corners.

red

Red is a colour. Tomatoes are red.

refrigerator

A **refrigerator** is a metal cupboard. It has a machine inside for keeping food cold.

repair

To **repair** something is to mend it.

reptile

A **reptile** is a cold-blooded animal with a backbone. Most reptiles are covered with scales. Snakes and lizards are reptiles.

lizard

snake

rescue

To **rescue** someone or something is to save them from danger or harm.

restaurant

A **restaurant** is a place where you can buy and eat a meal.

rhinoceros

A **rhinoceros** is a large, heavy animal with a thick skin. It has one or two horns on the top of its nose.

ribbon

A **ribbon** is a thin strip of material that you use to tie up gifts or hair.

rice

Rice is the small, white seeds of a plant that grows in wet ground in hot countries.

ride

To **ride** is to sit in or on something as it moves along. This girl is riding a horse.

right

Right is the opposite of left. This girl is making a right turn on her bicycle.

ring

When something **rings**, it makes the sound of a bell.

river

A **river** is a large stream of water that flows into another river, a lake, or the sea.

road

A **road** is a hard, smooth track for cars, lorries, and other traffic to drive on. There are many different types of roads.

ring

A **ring** is a circle of metal that you wear on your finger.

robot

A **robot** is a machine that can move and do some jobs that people can do.

rock

A **rock** is a large, heavy stone found in the ground.

rocket

A **rocket** is a metal tube full of gases. The gases make the power to send spacecraft into space.

roll

To **roll** is to turn over and over as you move along.

roof

A **roof** is the part that covers the top of a building.

room

A **room** is part of a building. A room has a **ceiling**, a **floor**, four **walls**, and a door.

root

A **root** is the part of a plant that grows underground. Roots take up water from the soil to feed the plant.

root

rope

Rope is strong, thick string. Ropes are used to pull or lift heavy things.

rose

A **rose** is a sweet-smelling flower with lots of petals, and thorns on its stem.

round

When something is **round**, it is shaped like a circle or a ball.

rug

A **rug** is a piece of material that covers part of a floor.

ruler

A **ruler** is a piece of wood that you use to draw and measure straight lines.

run

To **run** is to move very quickly on two legs.

runway

A **runway** is a strip of flat, smooth ground where aircraft can take off and land.

row

A **row** is a straight line of things.

Ss Ss Ss Ss

sad

A **sad** person is someone who feels unhappy.

saddle

A **saddle** is the seat you sit on when you ride on a horse.

sail

A **sail** is a large piece of material attached to a boat. Wind blows into the sails to move the boat through the water.

sail

To **sail** is to travel on a boat. A **sailor** is a person who works on a boat. A **sailing boat** is a boat that is moved along by wind in its sails.

salad

A **salad** is a cold mixture of vegetables like lettuce, radishes, and mushrooms.

salt

Salt is a white powder made from minerals found in sea water. Salt is used to flavour food.

same

When two things are the **same**, they are like each other in every way.

sand

Sand is grains of rock that cover a beach or desert.

sand-castle

sandwich

A **sandwich** is two pieces of bread with a tasty filling between them.

satellite

A **satellite** is any object that moves around a planet in space. Man-made satellites move around the Earth collecting information.

satellite dish

A **satellite dish** is a machine that receives information from a satellite.

saucepan

A **saucepan** is a metal container you use for cooking.

saw

A **saw** is a tool that has a blade with sharp, metal teeth. You use a saw to cut wood.

scale

A **scale** is a hard, thin piece of skin on a fish or a reptile. This fish is covered with hundreds of scales.

scales

Scales are a machine that is used to weigh things.

scarf

A **scarf** is a long piece of material worn around your neck.

school

A **school** is a place where you go to learn. At school your teacher teaches you important things such as how to read, write, and count.

scientist

A **scientist** is a person who studies a science like chemistry.

scissors

Scissors are a tool with two sharp blades. You use scissors to cut things.

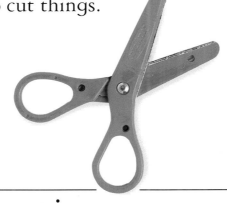

scorpion

A **scorpion** is an animal with two large claws and a poisonous sting in its tail.

scratch

To **scratch** yourself is to rub your skin with your fingernails to stop it from itching.

screw

A **screw** is a kind of nail with grooves.

scrub

To **scrub** is to rub something with a wet brush. This girl is scrubbing her nails.

sea

The **sea** is the part of the Earth that is salt water. Fish live in the sea.

seagull

A **seagull** is a sea bird with grey and white feathers.

seahorse

A **seahorse** is a fish with a head like a horse's head and a long tail.

seal

A **seal** is a large sea animal with grey fur and whiskers. Seals have flippers that help them to swim.

season

spring   summer

autumn   winter

A **season** is a time of year. There are four seasons and they always follow the same order: **spring**, **summer**, **autumn**, and **winter**.

seat-belt

A **seat-belt** is a safety strap in a vehicle. You wear a seat-belt around your body in case there is an accident.

seaweed

Seaweed is a plant that grows in the sea.

seed

A **seed** is the part of a plant that grows into a new plant.

seesaw

A **seesaw** is a balancing toy for two people. They sit at opposite ends of a long plank and rock up and down.

sell

To **sell** something is to give it to someone in return for money.

seven

Seven is the number that comes after six and before eight.

sew

To **sew** is to join material together using a needle and thread.

70

shadow

A **shadow** is a dark shape that you make when you stand in the way of light.

shark

A **shark** is a large sea animal with lots of big, sharp teeth.

shelf

A **shelf** is a long piece of wood that you keep things on.

shell

sea shell

A **shell** is the hard, outside covering of an egg, a nut, or an animal.

shake

To **shake** something is to move it quickly up and down and from side to side.

sharp

When something is **sharp**, it has an edge or a point that can cut things.

ship

A **ship** is a large boat that sails on the sea. Passenger ships carry people.

shape

A **shape** is the pattern you make when you draw round something. Circles, squares, triangles, and rectangles are all shapes.

sheep

A **sheep** is a farm animal with a thick, woolly coat. A female sheep is called a **ewe** and a male sheep is a **ram**.

shirt

A **shirt** is a garment that you wear on the top part of your body.

share

To **share** is to divide something into pieces and give some of it away. This boy is sharing his lunch with a friend.

shoe

A **shoe** is a strong covering for your foot. Shoes protect your feet from the hard ground.

shop

A **shop** is a building where you can buy things.

short

When something is **short**, it is not long.

shoulder

Your **shoulder** is the part of your body between your neck and arm.

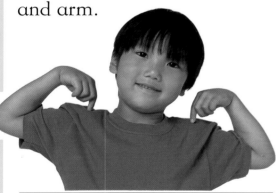

shout

To **shout** is to speak very loudly.

shower

A **shower** is a spray of water that you stand under to wash yourself.

shut

When something is **shut**, it is not open.

sing

To **sing** is to make music with your voice.

sink

When something **sinks**, it is too heavy to float and so it drops beneath the water.

sit

To **sit** is to rest your bottom on a chair or on the floor.

six

Six is the number that comes after five and before seven.

skate

To **skate** is to glide over ice wearing special boots with metal blades called **ice skates**.

skeleton

A **skeleton**
is an animal's
bones all
joined together.
You have a
skeleton inside
your body.

sky

The **sky** is the space above
your head where you can see
the sun and clouds.

slice

A **slice** is a thin piece of
something.

ski

To **ski**
is to slide
down snowy
mountains
wearing **skis**
on your feet.

skis

skyscraper

A **skyscraper**
is a very tall
building that
looks as if
it is touching
the sky.

slide

A **slide** is a kind of
toy. You climb to
the top of the
ladder and
drop down
a slippery
slope.

skip

To **skip** is to
jump over a
skipping rope
as it turns.
You can also
skip without
a rope.

sledge

A **sledge** is a vehicle made
out of wood with smooth,
metal runners on the
bottom. A sledge is used to
carry people over snow.

slow

When something is **slow**, it
takes a long time. This
tortoise is very slow to move
from one place to another.

sleep

To **sleep** is to close your eyes
and rest your body and
mind. You go to sleep at
night, or when you are tired.

small

When something is **small**,
it is little and not very big.

skirt

A **skirt** is a
garment that
hangs down
from the waist.

73

smile

When you **smile**, your face shows that you are happy.

snail

A **snail** is an animal with a soft body and a shell on its back.

snake

A **snake** is an animal with a long, thin body, a scaly skin, and no legs.

snow

Snow is tiny, white flakes of frozen water. Snow falls from clouds in cold weather.

snowman

A **snowman** is a model of a person made out of snow.

soap

Soap is a material that you use with water to wash away dirt.

soccer

Soccer is a ball game played by two teams of eleven players who kick a ball to score goals.

sock

A **sock** is a soft covering for your foot. You wear socks inside shoes.

sofa

A **sofa** is a long, cushioned seat with a back and arms. Two or three people can sit on a sofa.

soldier

A **soldier** is a person who is a member of an army.

solid

When something is **solid**, it keeps its shape and is firm and hard.

space

Space is the place above the Earth where there is no air. The planets are in space.

spacecraft

A **spacecraft** is a vehicle that travels in space.

spade

A **spade** is a tool that you use for digging. It has a long handle and a wide, flat blade.

sparrow

A **sparrow** is a small, brown bird. Sparrows are often seen in gardens.

spider

A **spider** is an animal with eight hairy legs. Spiders spin webs to catch small insects to eat.

spill

To **spill** something is to accidentally knock it out of its container.

spoon

A **spoon** is a tool that you use to pick up food.

sport

A **sport** is a game or a competition to exercise your body. There are lots of different sports like running and high jumping.

square

A **square** is a shape with four corners and four equal sides.

squash

To **squash** something is to press it and make it flat.

squeeze

To **squeeze** something is to press it. This girl is squeezing an orange.

squirrel

A **squirrel** is a furry animal with a long, bushy tail. Squirrels live in trees and eat nuts.

stable

A **stable** is a building for a horse to live in.

stamp

A **stamp** is a small piece of sticky paper that you put on an envelope. A stamp shows that you have paid to post a letter.

stand

To **stand** is to be on your feet without moving.

star

A **star** is one of the bright lights that shine in the sky at night.

starfish

A **starfish** is a sea animal with five arms that make the shape of a star.

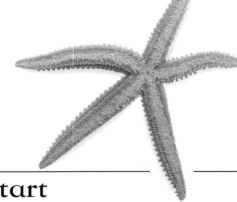

start

To **start** is to begin something. This boy is starting a race.

steering wheel

A **steering wheel** is the part of a car that you hold to turn the wheels.

stem

stem

A **stem** is the part of a plant from which the flowers and leaves grow.

stone

A **stone** is a small, hard piece of rock.

stopwatch

A **stopwatch** is a special kind of watch that you use to time a race.

strawberry

A **strawberry** is a small, red, juicy fruit.

stream

A **stream** is a small river.

string

String is a strong, thick thread that you use to tie things together.

stripe

A **stripe** is a narrow band of colour. This girl is wearing a striped T-shirt.

submarine

A **submarine** is a type of ship that travels underwater.

sugar

Sugar is a food sometimes made from sugar-cane. You use sugar to sweeten other foods.

sun

The **sun** is the huge, burning star that gives the Earth heat and light.

sunglasses

Sunglasses are dark glasses that you wear to protect your eyes from strong sunlight.

supermarket

A **supermarket** is a large shop that sells food and things for the house.

swan

A **swan** is a large water bird with a long neck and webbed feet.

swim

To **swim** is to move yourself through water using your arms and legs.

swimming pool

A **swimming pool** is a place where you swim.

swing

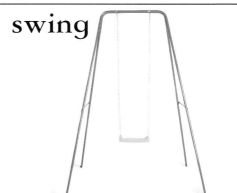

A **swing** is a hanging seat that you sit on and move backwards and forwards.

sword

A **sword** is a long, metal blade with a handle at one end.

synagogue

A **synagogue** is a building where Jewish people meet to pray.

T

Tt *Tt* **Tt** *Tt*

table

A **table** is a piece of furniture with a flat top and legs.

tadpole

A **tadpole** is a tiny animal that lives in a pond. Tadpoles grow into frogs.

tail

A **tail** is the part of an animal's body that sticks out at the back.

tall

When something is **tall**, it is higher than usual. The girl in the red T-shirt is taller than her friend.

tambourine

A **tambourine** is a round musical instrument with metal rings. You shake a tambourine to make a sound.

taxi

A **taxi** is a car that you travel in and then pay the driver.

tea

Tea is a drink made from the dried leaves of a tea-plant.

teacher

A **teacher** is a person who helps you to learn things.

team

A **team** is a group of people who work or play together.

tear

A **tear** is a drop of water that comes out of your eye.

tear

To **tear** something is to pull it apart.

telephone

A **telephone** is an instrument for talking to someone who is far away.

telescope

A **telescope** is an instrument that makes faraway objects look bigger and closer.

television

A **television** is a machine that receives messages sent through the air and turns them into sounds and pictures.

temple

A **temple** is a building where people go to pray.

ten

Ten is the number that comes after nine and before eleven.

tennis

Tennis is a game in which two or four players hit a ball, with a racket, over a net.

tent

A **tent** is a cloth shelter for camping in.

theatre

A **theatre** is a building where you go to see plays being acted on a stage.

thermometer

A **thermometer** is an instrument that measures how hot or cold something is. You can take your **temperature** with a thermometer.

thigh

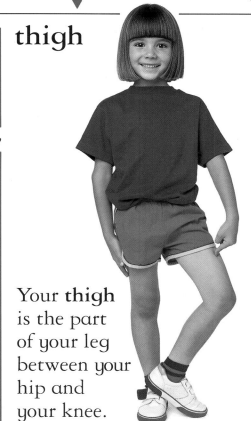

Your **thigh** is the part of your leg between your hip and your knee.

thin

When something is **thin**, it is not fat or thick.

thistle

A **thistle** is a prickly plant with a purple flower.

thorn

A **thorn** is a sharp point on the stem of some plants.

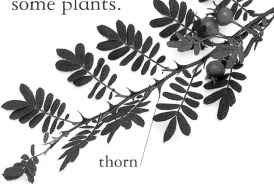

thorn

thread

A **thread** is a thin strand of cotton.

three

Three is the number that comes after two and before four.

tiger

A **tiger** is a wild, big cat with an orange and black striped coat.

thumb

Your **thumb** is the thick, short finger nearest to your wrist.

tile

A **tile** is a thin, flat covering for walls and floors.

tired

When you feel **tired**, you need to rest or sleep.

ticket

A **ticket** is a piece of paper that shows you have paid to travel on a bus or get into places like the theatre.

time

Time is a measurement in **hours**, **minutes**, and **seconds**.

toad

A **toad** is an animal that looks like a big frog with a rough, dry skin.

tie

A **tie** is a narrow strip of material that is tied around a shirt collar.

tiptoe

To **tiptoe** is to walk on your toes as quietly as you can.

toboggan

A **toboggan** is like a small, flat sledge. You can slide down snowy slopes on a toboggan.

tie

To **tie** something is to knot it together.

toe

Your **toe** is one of the five parts on the end of your foot.

toilet

A **toilet** is where you go to get rid of the waste in your body.

tomato

A **tomato** is a round, red fruit that you eat in salads.

tongue

Your **tongue** is the long, soft part inside your mouth. You can lick things with your tongue.

tool

A **tool** is an instrument that helps you to do a job. Spanners, screwdrivers, and pliers are all tools.

tooth

Your **tooth** is one of the white, bony parts in your mouth. You bite and chew with your **teeth**.

toothbrush

A **toothbrush** is a small brush that you use to clean your teeth. You put **toothpaste** on a toothbrush.

top

The **top** of something is the highest part of it. This boy is at the top of the slide.

tornado

A **tornado** is a very strong wind that whirls round and round. Tornados can rip up trees and knock down houses.

toucan

A **toucan** is a black and white bird with a large, brightly coloured beak.

tourist

A **tourist** is a person who visits places of interest.

towel

A **towel** is a piece of cloth you use to dry yourself with.

town

A **town** is a place with lots of houses, shops, and schools where people live and work.

toy

A **toy** is a plaything for you to have fun with.

tractor

A **tractor** is a farm machine that is used to pull heavy loads.

traffic

Traffic is all the cars, buses, motorbikes, and other vehicles that travel on the road.

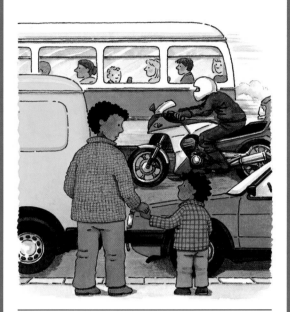

train

A **train** is a line of railway carriages that are pulled along a track by an engine. Trains carry passengers from one place to another.

transparent

When something is **transparent**, it is clear so that you can see through it. This glass jug is transparent.

trapeze

A **trapeze** is a type of swing that is used by acrobats.

tray

A **tray** is a flat piece of wood or plastic that you use to carry food and drink.

treasure

Treasure is gold, silver, coins, jewels, and other precious things. A treasure-chest is a box where you keep valuable objects.

tree

A **tree** is a large plant with leaves, branches, and a thick trunk.

triangle

A **triangle** is a shape with three straight sides and three corners.

trick

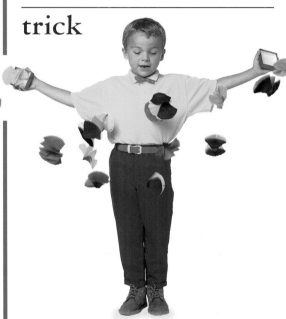

A **trick** is an amazing thing you can do to surprise people. This boy is pulling a lot of flowers out of a small box.

tricycle

A **tricycle** is a type of bicycle with three wheels.

trophy

A **trophy** is a large, metal cup that may be given as a prize.

trousers

Trousers are a piece of clothing that you wear on your legs.

truck

A **truck** is a big, powerful vehicle that is used to carry heavy loads. This truck has an open back for tipping out its load.

trumpet

valve

A **trumpet** is a musical instrument that is made out of brass. You blow into the mouthpiece and press the valves to make a sound.

trunk

A **trunk** is an elephant's long nose. Elephants use their trunks to squirt water into their mouths, and also to pick up things.

tugboat

A **tugboat** is a small, very powerful boat that is used to pull bigger boats in and out of harbour.

tulip

A **tulip** is a cup-shaped flower that grows from a bulb and blooms in the spring.

tunnel

A **tunnel** is a long passage cut through a hill or under the ground.

turkey

A **turkey** is a large, farm bird with black and white feathers and a long, red chin.

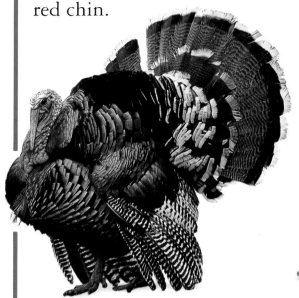

turtle

A **turtle** is a sea animal with a scaly body covered by a hard shell. Turtles live on land and in water.

tusk

A **tusk** is the long, pointed tooth of an elephant.

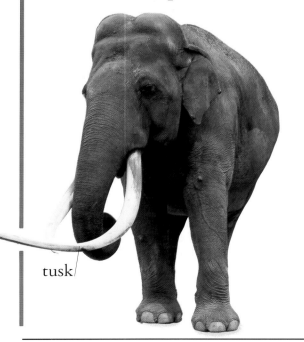

tusk

twig

A **twig** is a small, thin branch of a tree. Leaves grow on twigs.

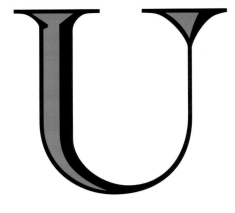

twin

A **twin** is one of two children that were born at the same time to the same parents.

two

Two is the number that comes after one and before three.

typewriter

A **typewriter** is a machine with keys that you press to print letters and numbers onto paper.

U

Uu *Uu* Uu *Uu*

umbrella

An **umbrella** is a piece of waterproof material on a frame. An umbrella keeps you dry when it rains.

under

To be **under** something is to be below it. The toy soldier is standing under the arch.

underwear

Underwear is clothing that you wear next to your skin, under your other clothes.

undress

To **undress** is to take off your clothes. You undress to get ready for bed.

unicorn

A **unicorn** is an imaginary animal. It looks like a horse with a long, twisted horn on its forehead.

university

A **university** is a place where you can go to learn after leaving school.

up

When something goes **up**, it moves to a higher place. This girl is throwing the ball up into the air.

V

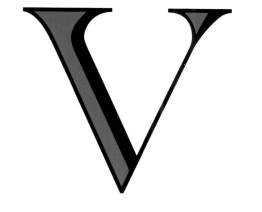

Vv *Vv* Vv *Vv*

vacuum cleaner

A **vacuum cleaner** is a machine that sucks up dirt from the floor.

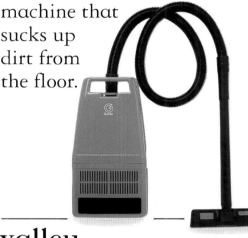

valley

A **valley** is the low land between two hills.

vase

A **vase** is a container for holding cut flowers.

vegetable

A **vegetable** is a plant with roots or leaves that you can eat either cooked or raw. There are lots of different kinds of vegetables.

vehicle

A **vehicle** is a machine that carries people and things from one place to another. Cars and trucks are vehicles.

vet

A **vet** is a type of doctor who cares for animals when they are sick or injured.

videotape

A **videotape** is a recording of pictures and sounds. You use a **videotape recorder** and a television to watch a videotape.

violin

A **violin** is a musical instrument made out of wood. You hold it under your chin and draw a bow across its strings.

bow

WwWwWwWw

village

A **village** is a small group of houses and shops in the countryside.

volcano

A **volcano** is a mountain with a hole in the top. Sometimes hot melted rocks, gas, and ash burst out of a volcano.

wagon

A **wagon** is a cart that is used to carry heavy loads. Wagons are sometimes pulled by horses.

waiter

A **waiter** is a person who serves food and drink in a restaurant.

vine

A **vine** is a climbing plant. Grapes grow on vines in fields called **vineyards**.

vulture

A **vulture** is a large bird with a bald head. Vultures eat dead animals.

walk

To **walk** is to move along on your feet.

walking stick

A **walking stick** is a long, thin piece of wood that you use to help you to walk.

wallaby

A **wallaby** is a small, furry animal that jumps like a kangaroo.

wallet

A **wallet** is a small, flat case that you keep your money in.

walrus

A **walrus** is a big sea animal with a large body and two long, curved tusks.

wash

To **wash** is to clean yourself with soap and water.

watch

To **watch** something is to look at it carefully.

watch

A **watch** is a small clock that you wear on your wrist.

water

 Water is the clear liquid that comes out of a tap. Water falls from the sky as rain.

waterfall

A **waterfall** is a stream or river flowing over the edge of a rock.

waterlily

A **waterlily** is a flower that grows in ponds and lakes.

watermelon

A **watermelon** is a large fruit with a red, watery inside.

wave

To **wave** is to move your hand and signal hello or goodbye.

wear

To **wear** something is to put it on. This boy is wearing a hat on his head and clothes on his body.

wedding

A **wedding** is a special time when two people get married.

week

A **week** is a measurement of time that is seven days long. There are fifty-two weeks in one year.

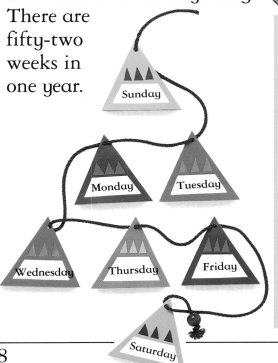

weigh

To **weigh** something is to find out how heavy it is.

wet

When something is **wet**, it is covered with water and is not dry. This dog is very wet and is shaking himself dry.

whale

A **whale** is a huge sea animal that breathes air. Whales are the largest living animals.

wheat

Wheat is a plant that is grown on a farm. We grind wheat to make flour.

wheel

A **wheel** is a round frame that turns on a rod in order to move things.

wheelbarrow

A **wheelbarrow** is a small cart with a wheel at the front. It can be used to move things like soil and stones.

wheelchair

A **wheelchair** is a special chair that you move about in if you have difficulty walking.

whiskers

Whiskers are the long hairs that grow on an animal's face.

whisper

To **whisper** is to talk very quietly so that only one person can hear you.

whistle

A **whistle** is an instrument that makes a sharp, high sound when you blow it.

white

White is a colour. Snow and salt are white.

wide

When something is **wide**, it measures a lot from one side to the other.

wind

The **wind** is air that is moving quickly.

windmill

A **windmill** is a machine that uses the power of the wind to turn its sails. Wheat is ground into flour in a windmill.

window

A **window** is an opening in a wall that is filled with a pane of glass. Windows let in light and air.

wing

wing

Wings are the part of an animal that help it to fly.

wire

Wire is a thin, metal thread that is often covered with plastic.

witch

A **witch** is an imaginary woman with magical powers.

wizard

A **wizard** is an imaginary man with magical powers.

wolf

A **wolf** is a wild animal that looks like a large, fierce dog.

woman

A **woman** is a grown-up girl.

wood

Wood is the hard part of a tree that is used to make tables and chairs.

wool

Wool is the soft, curly hair of a sheep. Wool is spun into yarn and used for knitting or making cloth.

world

The **world** is the Earth and everything that lives on it.

worm

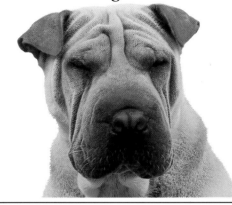

A **worm** is a long animal that lives in the ground.

wrinkle

A **wrinkle** is a crease in the skin. This dog has wrinkles.

wrist

Your **wrist** is the joint between your hand and your arm.

write

To **write** is to put words on paper so that people can read them.

X

Xx Xx Xx Xx

X-ray

An **X-ray** is a special photograph of the inside of your body. Doctors can look at an X-ray to find out if you are sick or injured.

xylophone

A **xylophone** is a musical instrument that is made of metal or wooden bars. You hit the bars with beaters to make musical sounds.

Y

Yy *Yy* Yy Yy

yacht

A **yacht** is a fast sailing boat with a cabin.

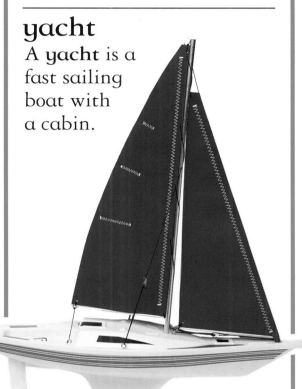

yawn

To **yawn** is to open your mouth wide and breathe in deeply. You yawn when you are tired.

year

A **year** is a measure of time that lasts 12 months, 52 weeks, or 365 days.

yellow

Yellow is a colour. Lemons are yellow.

yoghurt

Yoghurt is a thick, creamy food made from milk. Yoghurt often has fruit in it.

yolk

A **yolk** is the yellow part of an egg.

young

A **young** person is someone who is only a few years old. This baby is young.

Z

Zz Zz Zz Zz

zebra

A **zebra** is an animal that looks like a horse with black and white stripes on its body.

zero

Zero is the number that comes before one. Zero means nothing.

zip

A **zip** is a fastener for clothes.

zoo

A **zoo** is a place where wild animals are kept for people to visit and learn about.

Dictionary games

See if you can solve all these word puzzles, using your dictionary to help you. At the same time, you can practise looking up words and spellings. You will find all the answers to the puzzles somewhere in the dictionary. The pictures will help you to find the word you are looking for more easily.

Every puzzle has a special, helpful box with the first question answered for you, so that you can see what to do. Remember to write your answers down on a piece of paper, not in the book! You can play most of the games on your own, but sometimes you will need a friend to help you. Have fun!

Animal alphabet

These animals should be in alphabetical order, but they have got all mixed up. Use the alphabet at the top of the page to help you to sort them out.

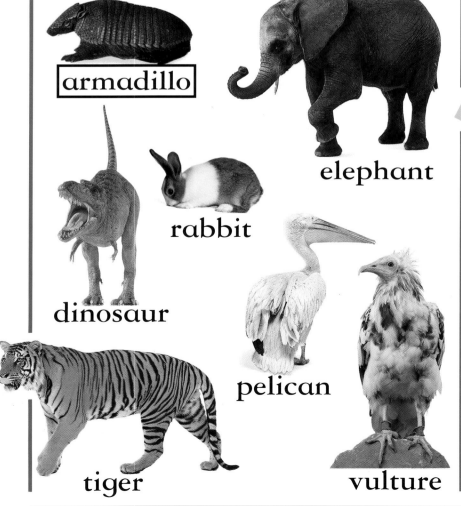

armadillo

elephant

rabbit

dinosaur

pelican

tiger

vulture

Spelling puzzle

You probably know the names of a lot of these pictures, but can you spell them? Have a go first, and then use your dictionary to see how many you got right.

acrobat

c

p

y

e

s

w

d

d

Word detective

Find the right word to answer these questions. You can use the clues to help you, just like a detective does.

> • What do you call a person who breaks into a building to steal something?
> The word begins with the letter **b**.
> ## burglar

• What is the name for precious things like gold, silver, coins, and jewels?
Look for the things that sparkle on page 82.

• What can you wear over your face to disguise yourself?
Find the hidden face under **m**.

• What do you call a person who keeps law and order?
Look for a word beginning with **p**.

• What does a detective use to find the clues left behind by a burglar?
Try page 47.

Dictionary lucky dip

Here is a game that you can play on your own or with a friend.

1) Think of a letter of the alphabet.

2) Now, close your dictionary and try to open it again at exactly the right place to find the letter you have chosen.

You score two points if you find the correct page, and one point if you are near.

Test your memory

Look carefully at all the objects below for one minute. Next, close the dictionary and see how many things you can remember.
Write them down, and then try arranging the words in alphabetical order to make your own little dictionary.

Odd one out

If you look carefully at the things below, you will see that in each group there is an "odd one out". Can you find out which one it is by reading the dictionary definitions?

snake   beetle   bee

The **snake** is the odd one out because it is not an insect.

crown   glove   hat

grape   pear   carrot

trumpet   recorder   violin

Find that word

Use the index at the back of this book to help you to find the answers to these questions. Look for each word in **bold** type in the index, and it will tell you the page number you want.

- What do you do in a **cinema**? You watch a film in a cinema.

- Who do **guide dogs** help?

- What is a **stallion**?

- How do **fire fighters** travel to a fire?

- Why do people send out **invitations**?

- Is there another word for a **rainforest**?

- **Mars** is a planet, can you name any others?

Sound-alikes

Some words sound the same when you say them, but they have different meanings. With a friend, say these words out loud, and then take it in turns to look up the meanings. Do you know more pairs of words like this?

bat A **bat** is a kind of stick that you use to hit a ball.	**bat** A **bat** is a small, furry animal with wings.
cricket	cricket
flour	flower
nut	nut
orange	orange
pair	pear
right	write
tie	tie

Animal jumble

On this page you can see lots of animals that are all jumbled up. Answer the questions to find out which animals make pairs or sets. Remember that the dictionary definitions will help you.

Which of these birds cannot fly?

toucan

sheep

jaguar

dog

dolphin

crab

lamb

ostrich

How many of these birds can swim?

Can you match the mothers with their babies?

gosling

kitten

penguin

starfish

Which of these animals live in, or around, water?

goose

cat

There are three cats on this page. Can you point to them?

puppy

crocodile

Index of additional words

Acknowledgements

Dorling Kindersley would like to thank the following people for their assistance in the production of this book:

Senior editor Nicola Tuxworth
Senior art editor Rowena Alsey
Jacket design Christopher Branfield
Picture research Jenny Rayner and Sarah Moule
Additional design Mark Richards, Nicky Simmonds, and Sharon Peters

Picture Agency Credits
t=top; b=bottom; l=left; r=right; c=centre
Aquila/A. Cooper 22tr; Bruce Coleman Ltd./E. & P. Bauer 84tl, M. Freeman 19cb, L. Lee Rue 37clb, M.P. Kahl 16bl, H. Reinhard 26crt, K. Tanaka (WWF) 55br; FLPA/E. & D. Hosking 42br, 87bl; NHPA/O. Rogge 24clt; OSF/J. A. L. Cooke 50clt; Science Photo Library/T. Craddock 68br; Survival Anglia/M. Day 33tl.

Additional Photography
Simon Battensby, Jon Boucher, Paul Bricknell, Jane Burton, Peter Chadwick, Gordon Clayton, Antony Cooper, Geoff Dann, Philip Dowell, Michael Dunning, Andreas Einsiedel, Jo Foord, Philip Gatward, Paul Goff, Frank Greenaway, Stephen Hayward, Colin Keates, Dave King, Bob Langrish, Cyril Laubscher, Ray Moller, David Murry, Stephen Oliver, Daniel Pangbourne, Roger Philips, Suzanna Price, Karl Shone, Steve Shott, Clive Streeter, Kim Taylor, Mathew Ward, Paul Williams, Jerry Young.

Models
Abdul Matin, Stacy Afrakumah, Alex Arthur, Peter Ballingall, Daryl Belsey, Mark Belsey, Penny Britchfield, Geoff Boyd, Simona Businaro, Lotte Butler, Vanessa Chadwick, Lois Chapman, Amanda Choudhury, Gemmel Cole, Gregory Coleman, Bobby Cooper, Andy Crawford, Sharon Daley-Johnson, Mandy Earey, Hugo Edwards, Karen Edwards, Saphire Elia, David Gillingwater, Kashi Gorton, Steve Gorton, Miranda Hutcheon, Rebecca Kern, Jane Latchford, Fiona McKenzie, Kensuke Miyoshi, Julian Morris, Nicola Naylor, Earl Neish, Lian Ng, Martin Pamphillon, Hiral Patel, Maxwell Ralph, Charlotte Raynsford, Tim Ridley, Elizabeth Robert, Jenifer Rogers, Stacy Ryan, Nicky Simmonds, Francis Taylor, John Waldon, Elizabeth Wilkes, Nagisa Yamagami, Yan-kit So.

Additional Acknowledgements
Sarah Ashun and Agry Ombler - photographer's assistants; Sue Wookey - picture research; Guide Dogs for the Blind; Great Ormond Street Hospital for the crutches; Design Studio, Reigate, for the tile; James Smith & Sons (Umbrellas) Ltd. for the walking stick; The Bead Shop, Covent Garden, for the treasure; Nigel Busch for the motorbike; Rank Film Distributors Ltd. for the film; Kentish Town City Farm for supplying the cow and calf for photography; Frank Barnes School, Julians Primary School, and Columbia Road Primary School for permitting their pupils to appear in the book; pupils and teachers of Winnersh Primary School, The Coombes at Arborfield, and Columbia Road Primary School for field-testing the pages of **My First Dictionary** during production.